Well-Tempered Blues
8 NEW BLUES TUNES FOR CLASSICAL & FINGERSTYLE GUITAR

BY WILLIAM BEAUVAIS

www.melbay.com/99967BCDEB

Audio Contents

1 Drinking Water Blues [2:42]	5 Gridlock Blues [3:14]
2 Twisted Fingers [1:43]	6 Rainy Weekend Blues [1:47]
3 Deep Down Blues [2:58]	7 Snaky Blue Line [2:42]
4 Cutback Blues [1:40]	8 Chicago Style Blues [3:46]

© 2004 BY MEL BAY PUBLICATIONS, INC.
ALL RIGHTS RESERVED.INTERNATIONAL COPYRIGHT SECURED. MADE AND PRINTED IN U.S.A.
No part of this publication may be reproduced in whole or in part, or stored in a retrieval system, or transmitted in any form
or by any means, electronic, mechanical, photocopy, recording, or otherwise, without written permission of the publisher.

Visit us at www.melbay.com — E-mail us at email@melbay.com

Preface

Well Tempered Blues is a collection of twelve bar blues pieces. I have sometimes used the baroque style of notation: writing a single line to make the music and rhythms more obvious. In these cases, such as "Chicago Style Blues" and "Twisted Fingers," try leaving the bass notes down as long as possible, and let your ear tell you what sounds the best. Slides have not been indicated but have been left for the player to decide. Try sliding into various notes and choose what sounds the best. There is a great deal of room for flexibility in these pieces. Some people have also suggested that these pieces can be used for jamming, with an improviser adding a solo line over the guitar part.

Blues is a style that demands that the player be deeply expressive. Every note can be colored with pitch bends, slides, vibrato and all manner of attacks. In tastefully adding these nuances, a player begins to own the music, to make it their own, to play each piece as if they wrote it. These pieces are designed to be fun, and entertaining as they work through the keys that are most idiomatic to the guitar.

Table of Contents

Drinking Water Blues 4

Twisted Fingers 9

Deep Down Blues 14

Cutback Blues 19

Gridlock Blues 24

Rainy Weekend Blues 30

Snaky Blue Line 36

Chicago Style Blues 41

About the Author 47

Drinking Water Blues
for Cassandra

William Beauvais

Moderate, with feeling
♩.=112

© 2004 by Mel Bay Publications, Inc. All Rights Reserved.

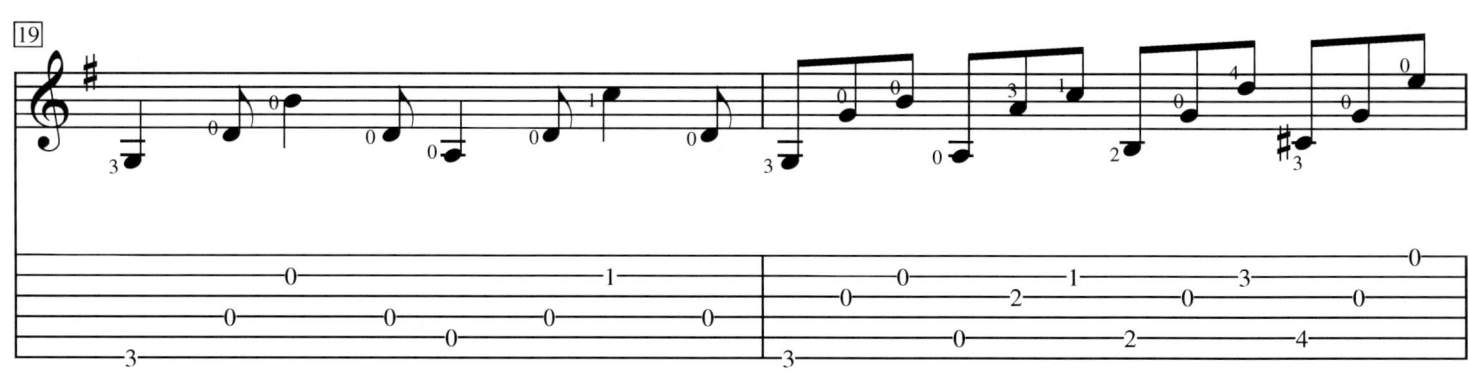

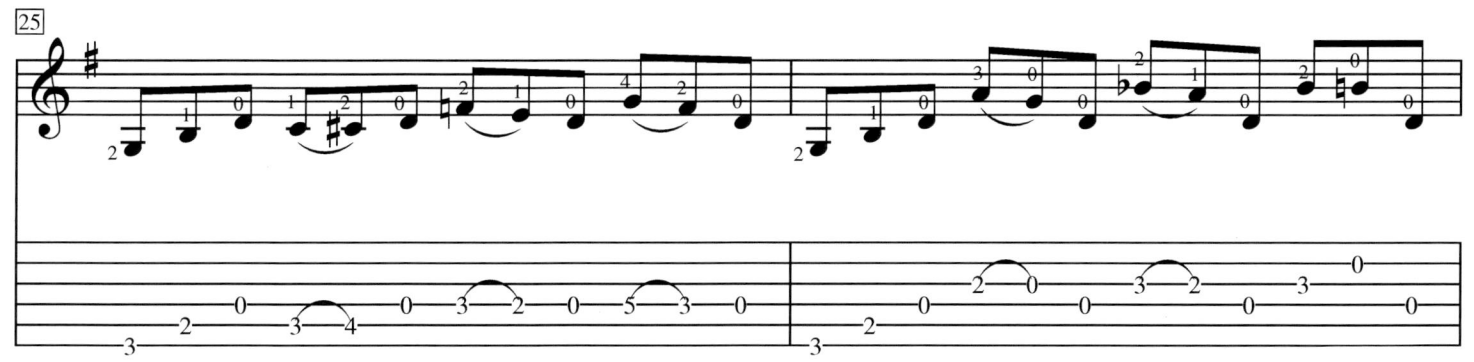
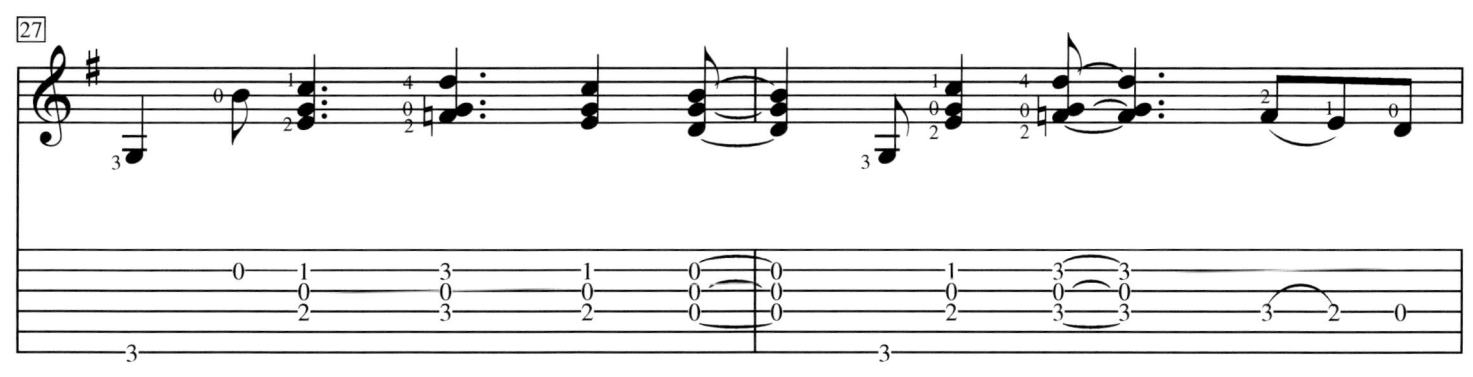
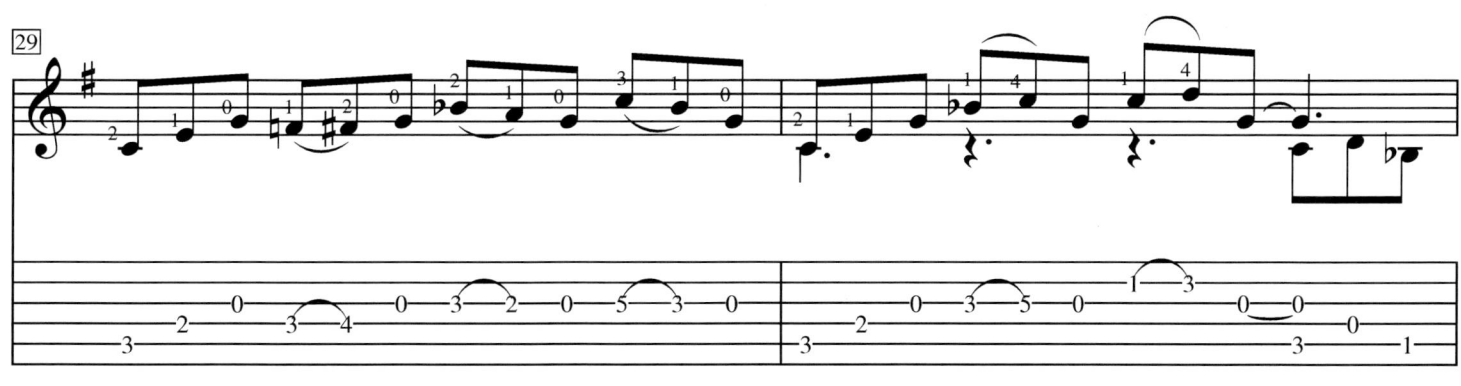

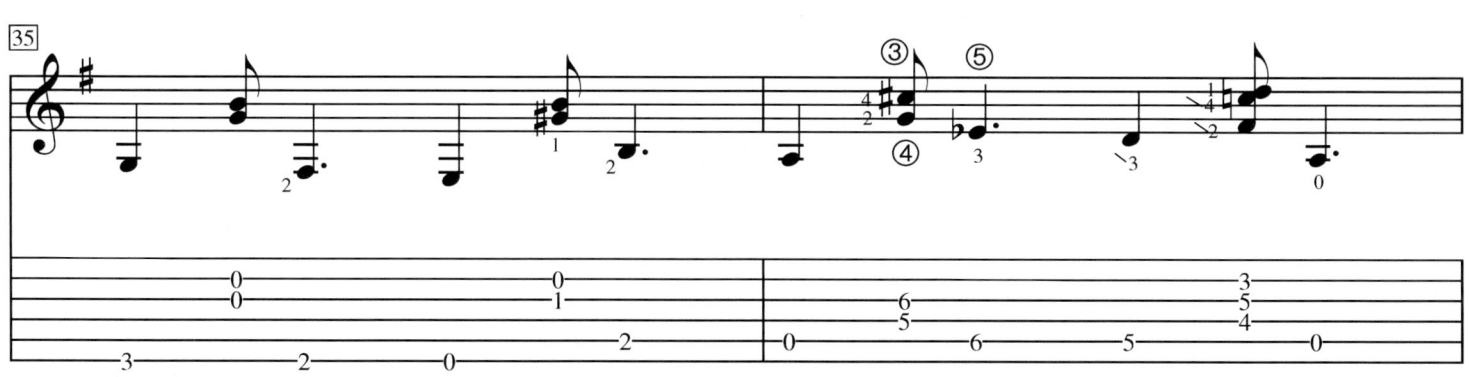
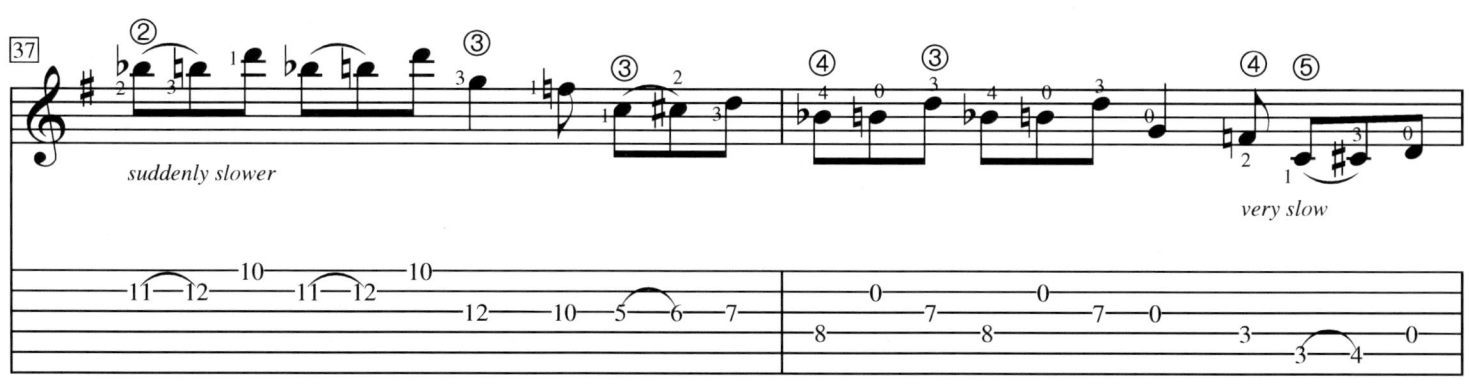

Twisted Fingers
for Gary Gontier

William Beauvais

Moderate, rock groove
♩.=124

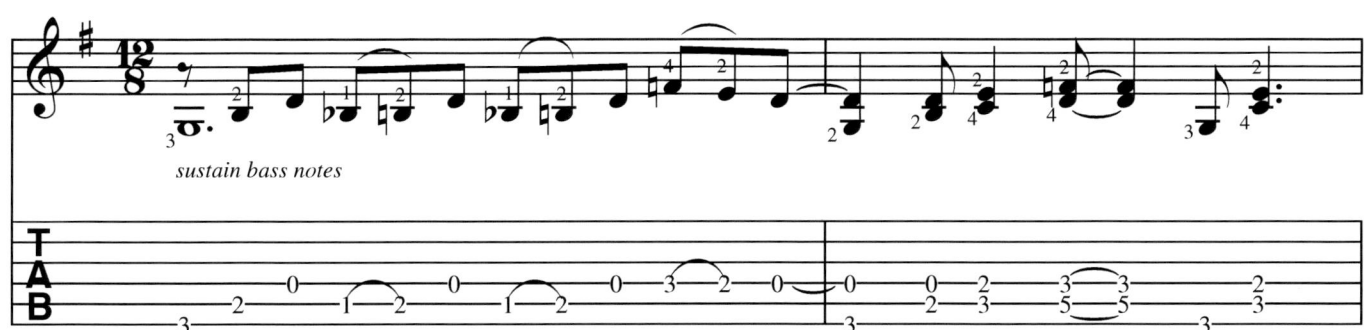
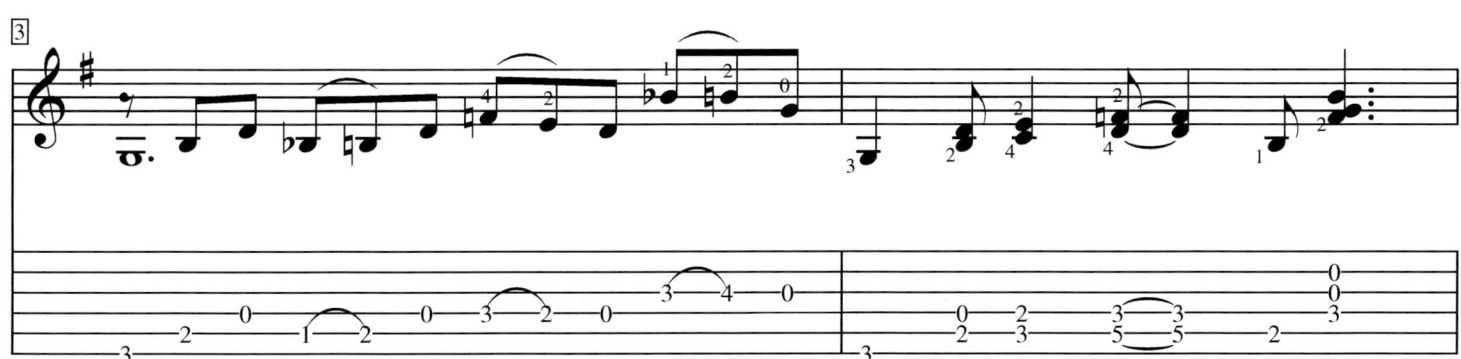

© 2004 by Mel Bay Publications, Inc. All Rights Reserved.

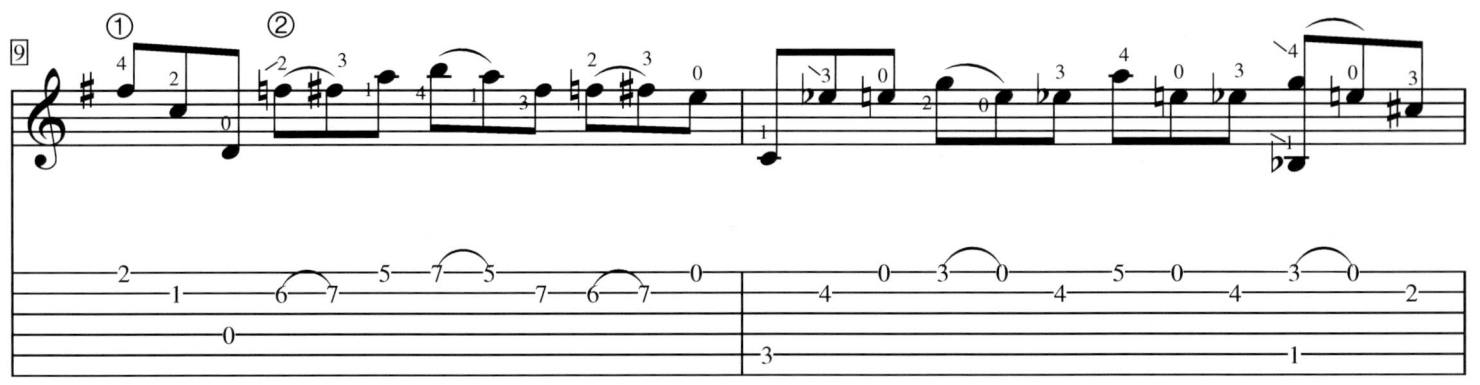
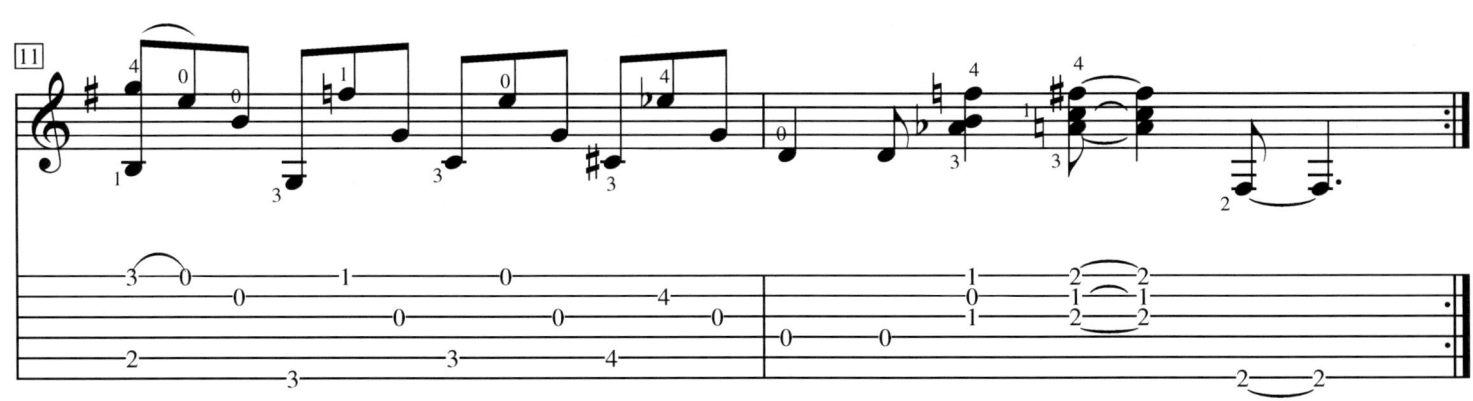

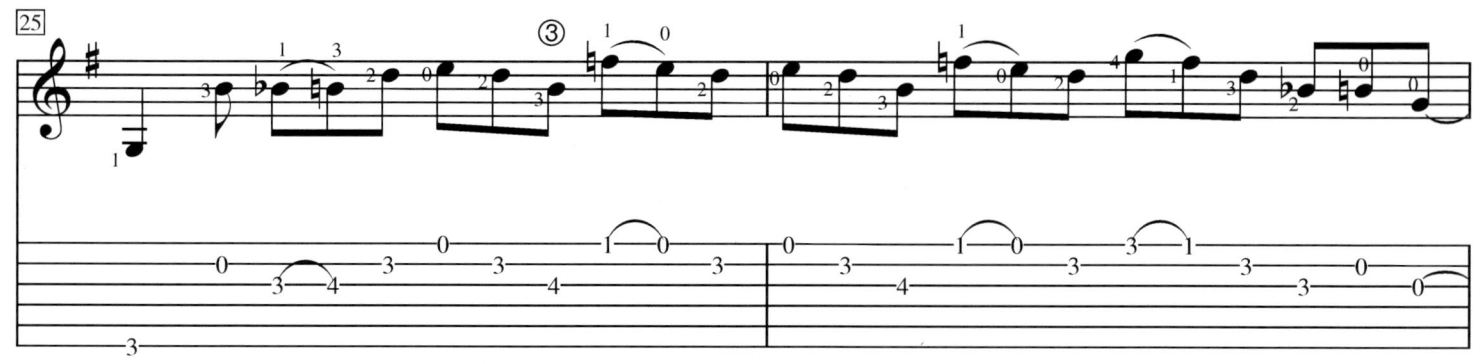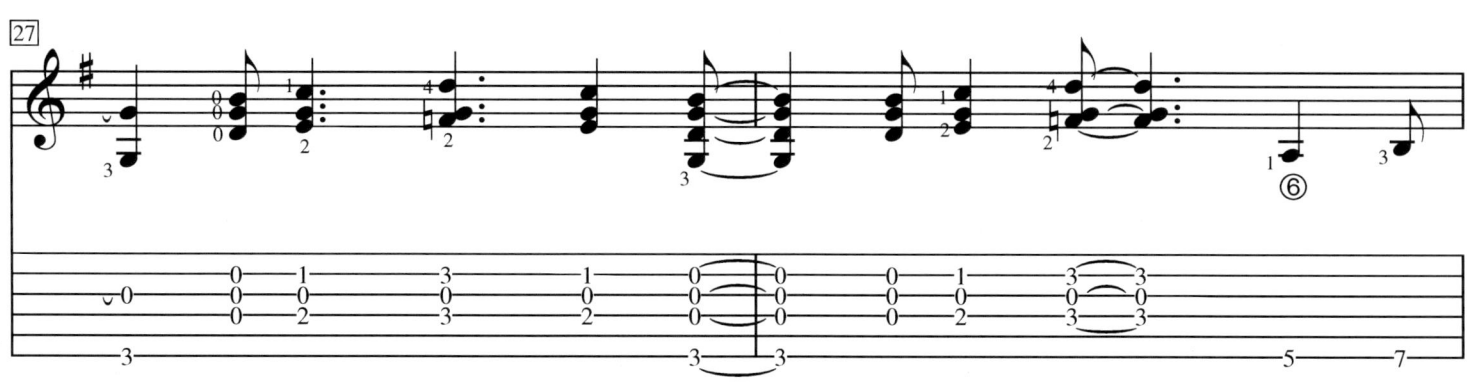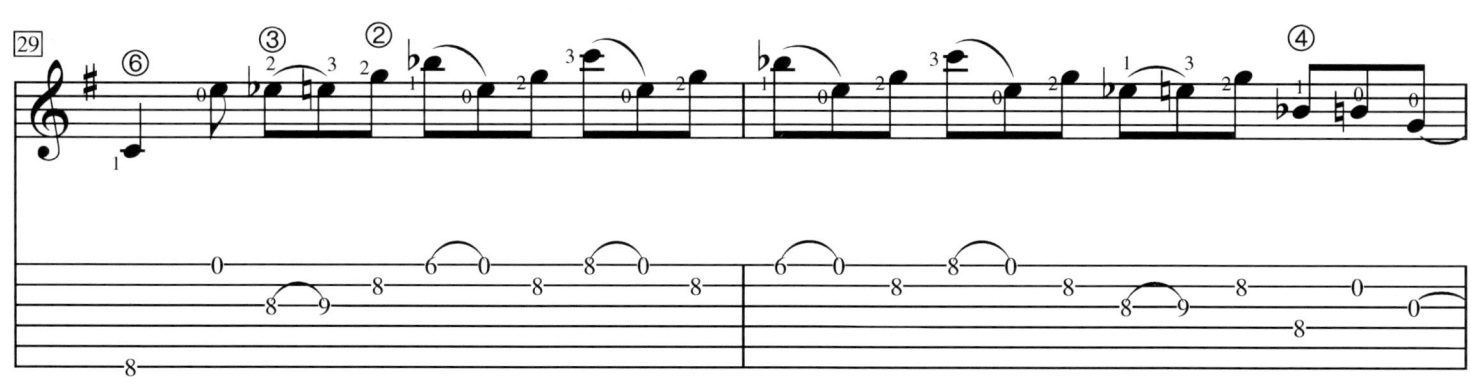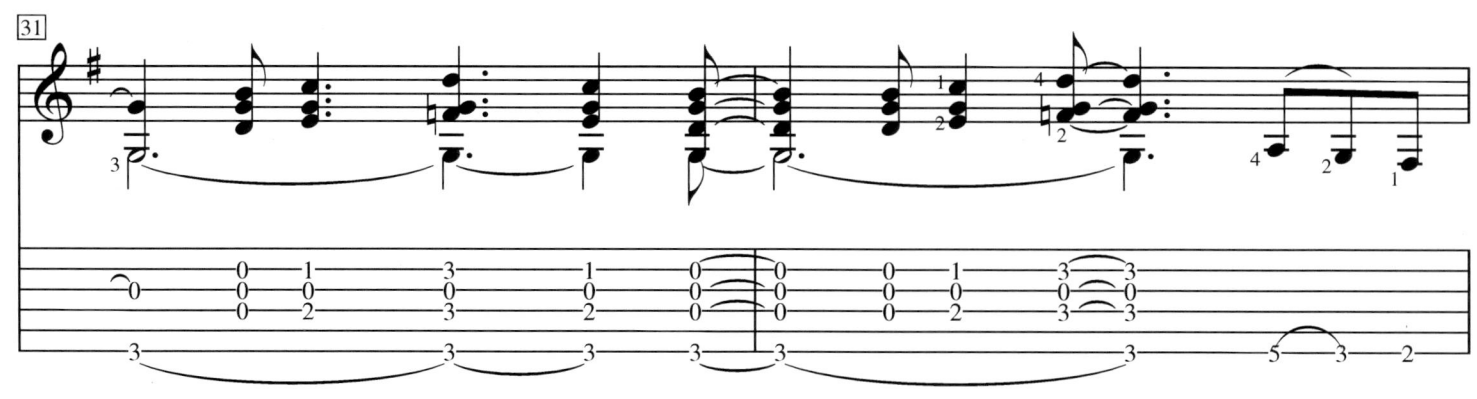

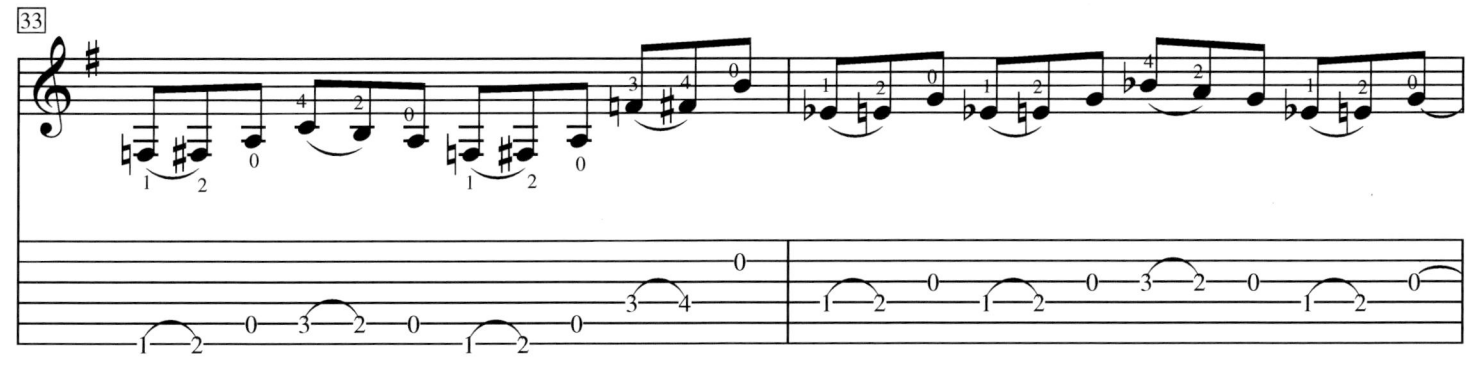
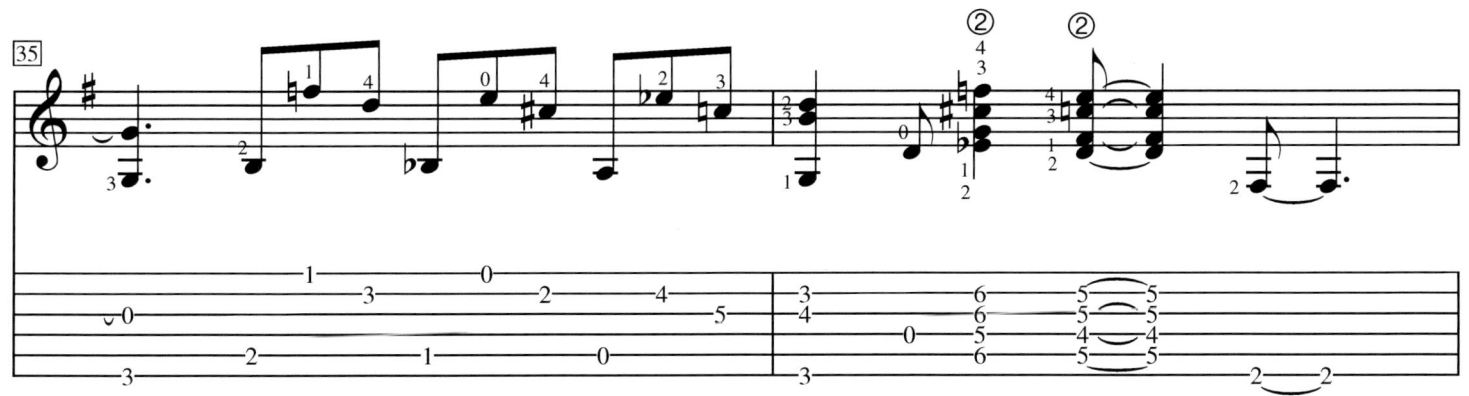
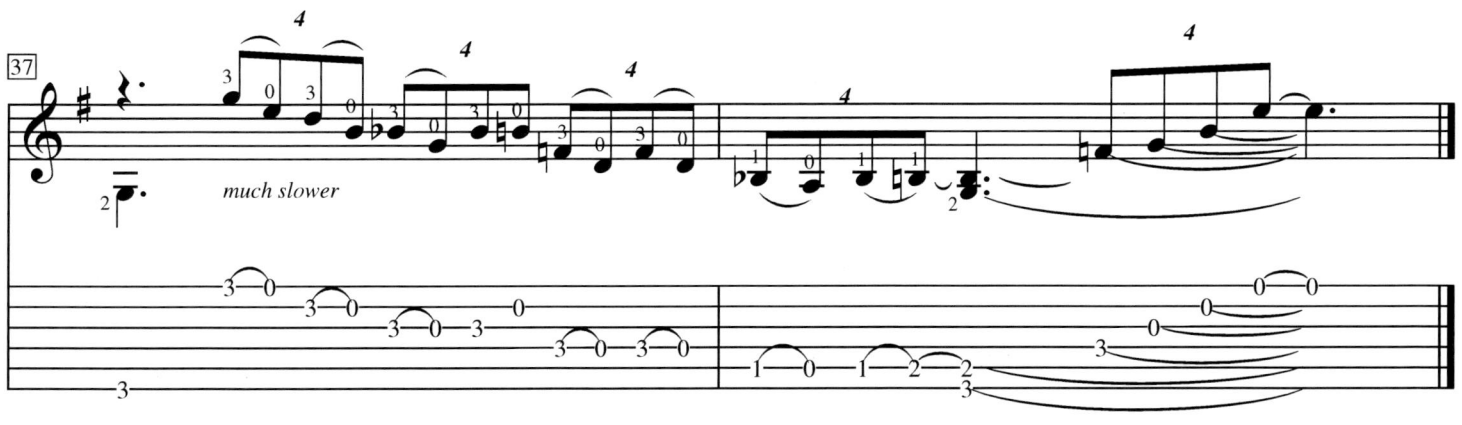

much slower

Deep Down Blues
for Marcello Colonel

William Beauvais

Slow, rock groove
⑥=D ♩.=64

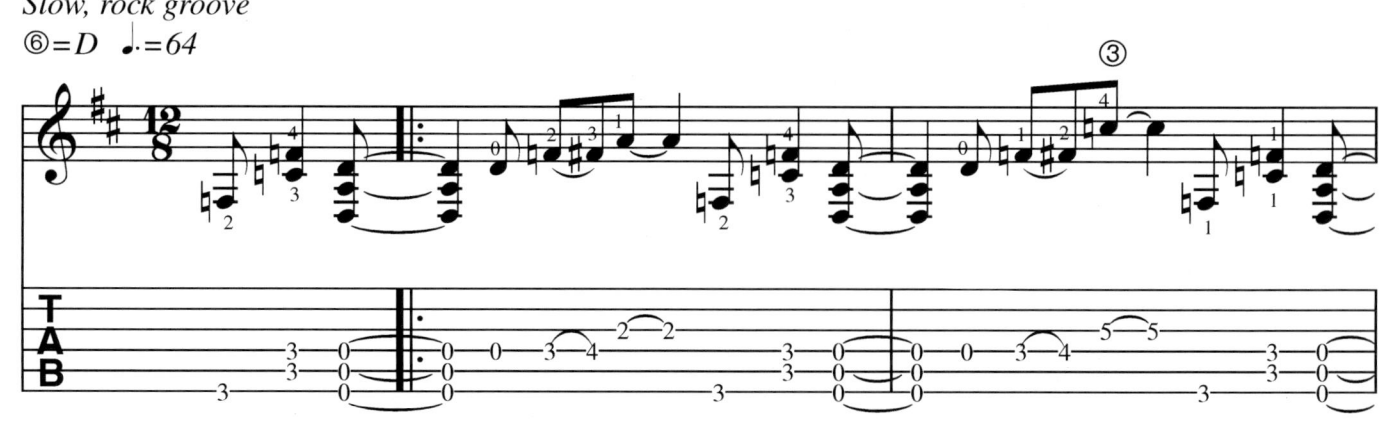

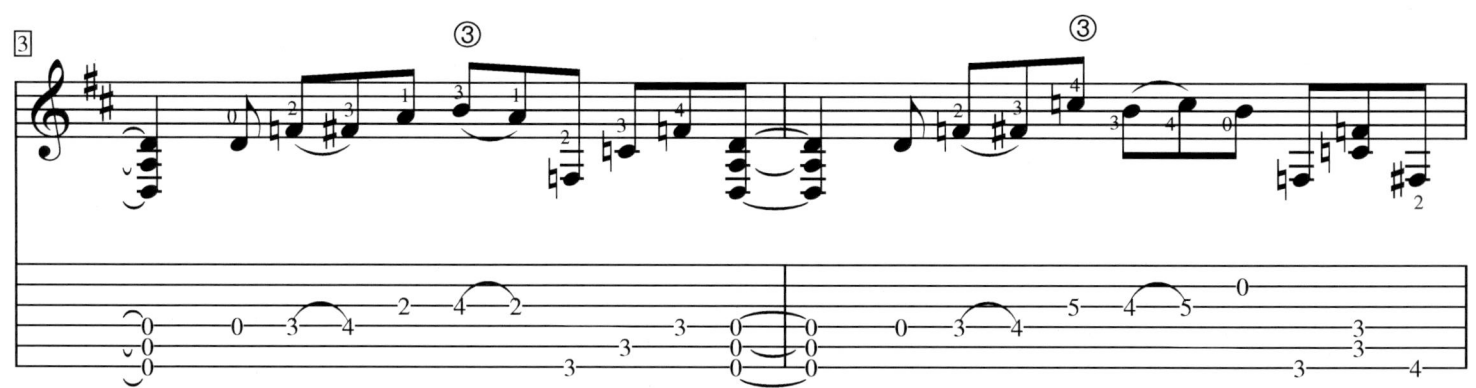

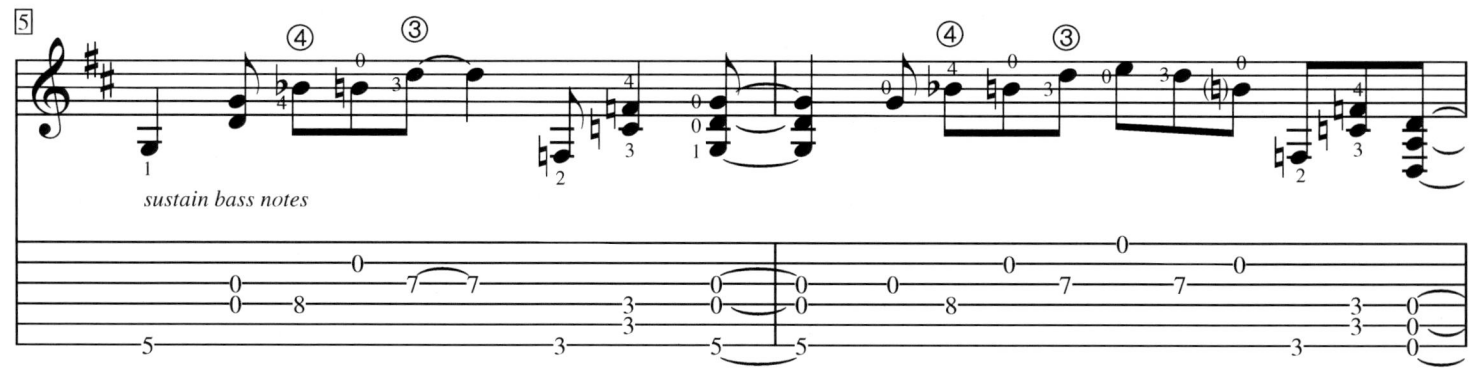

sustain bass notes

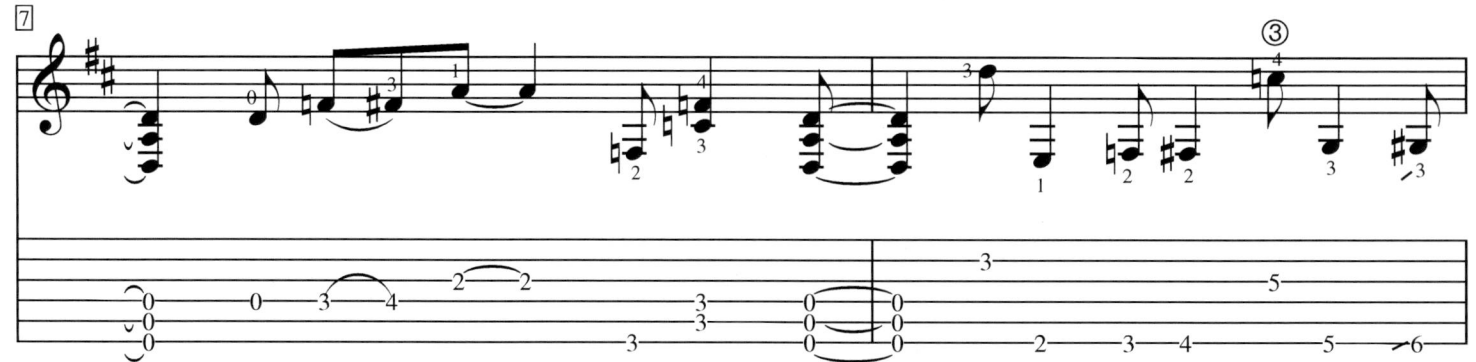

© 2004 by Mel Bay Publications, Inc. All Rights Reserved.

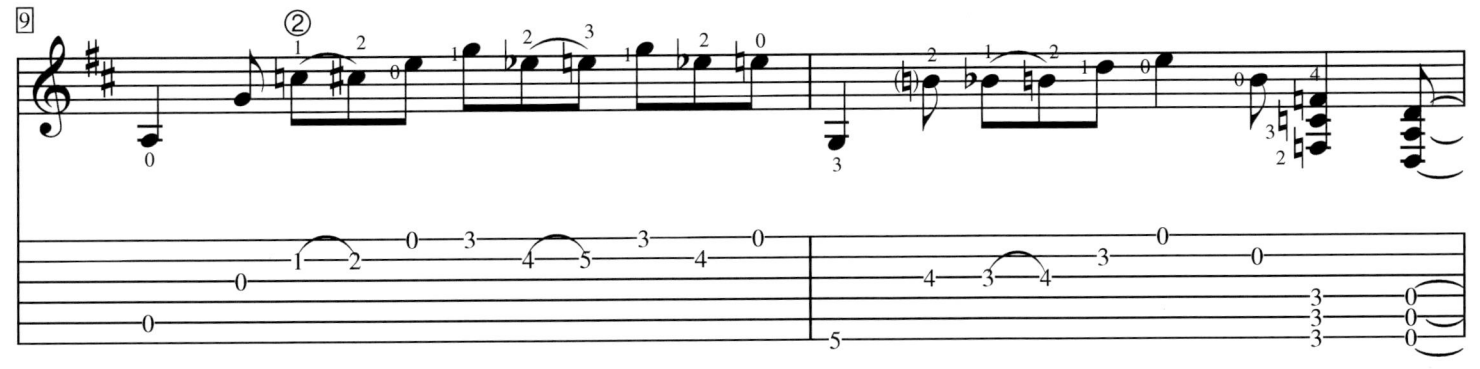

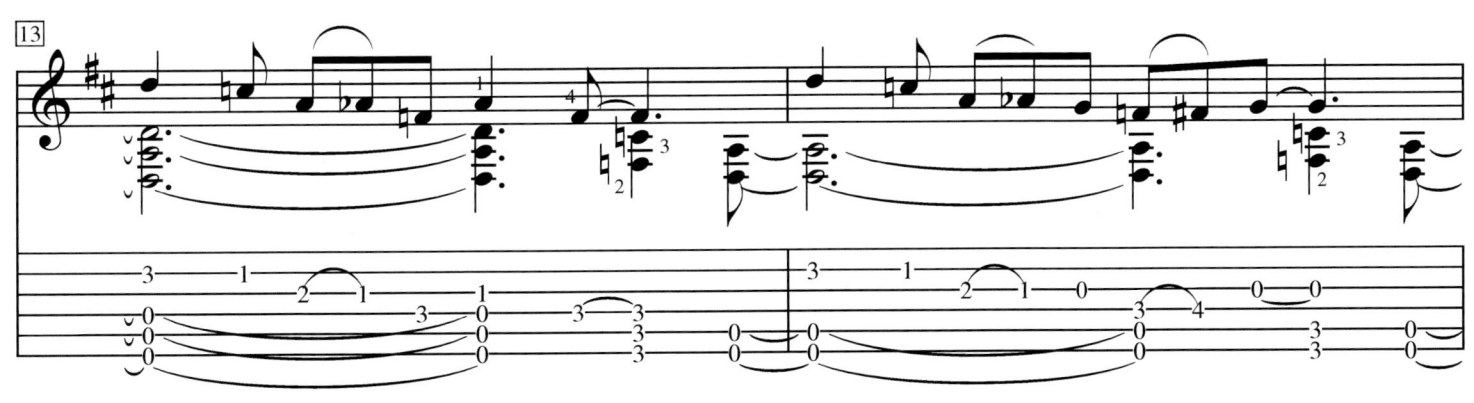

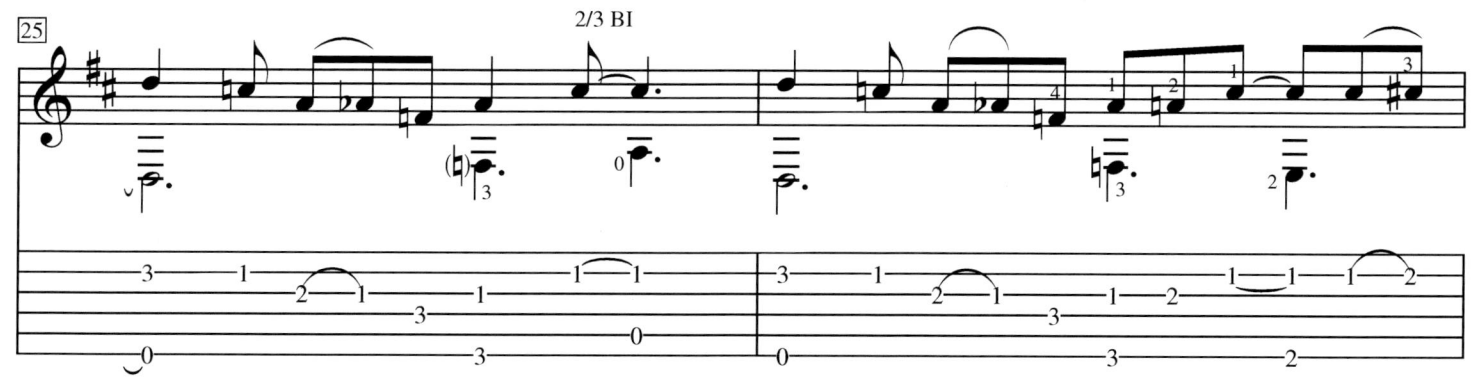
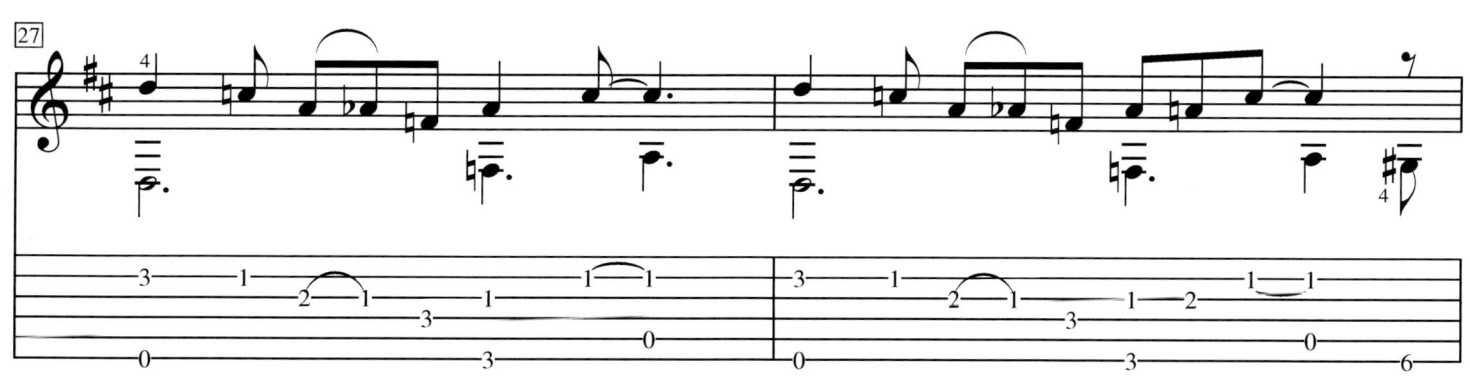

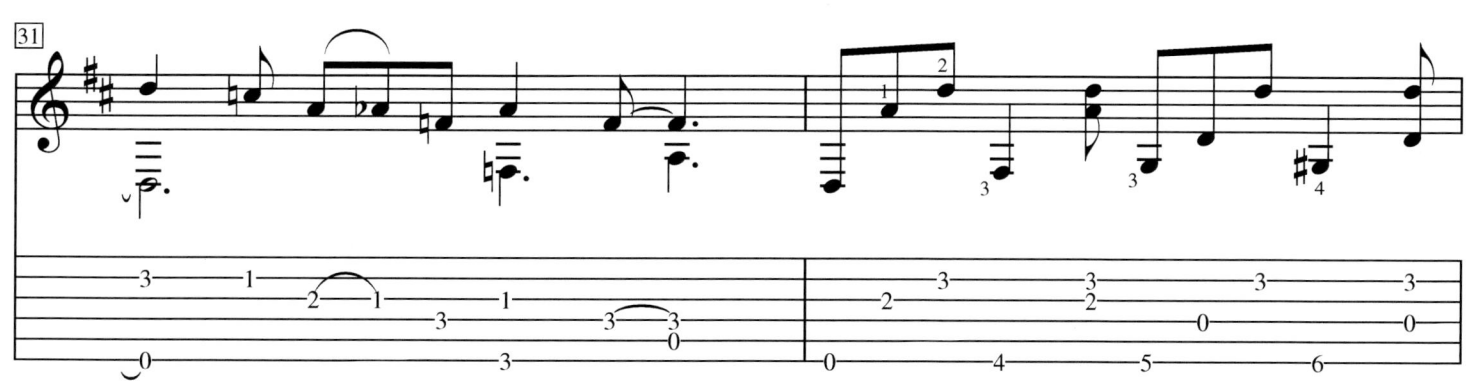

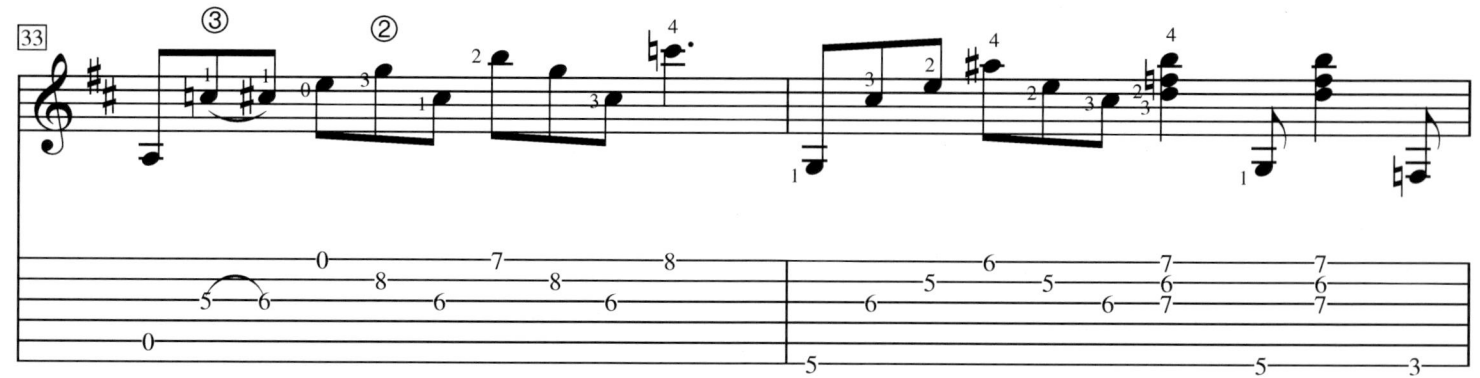
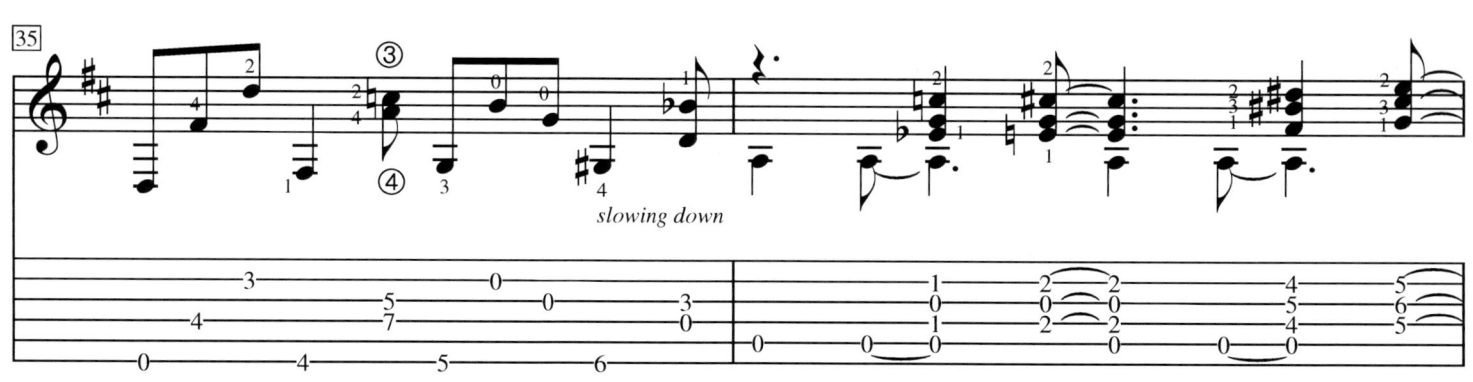
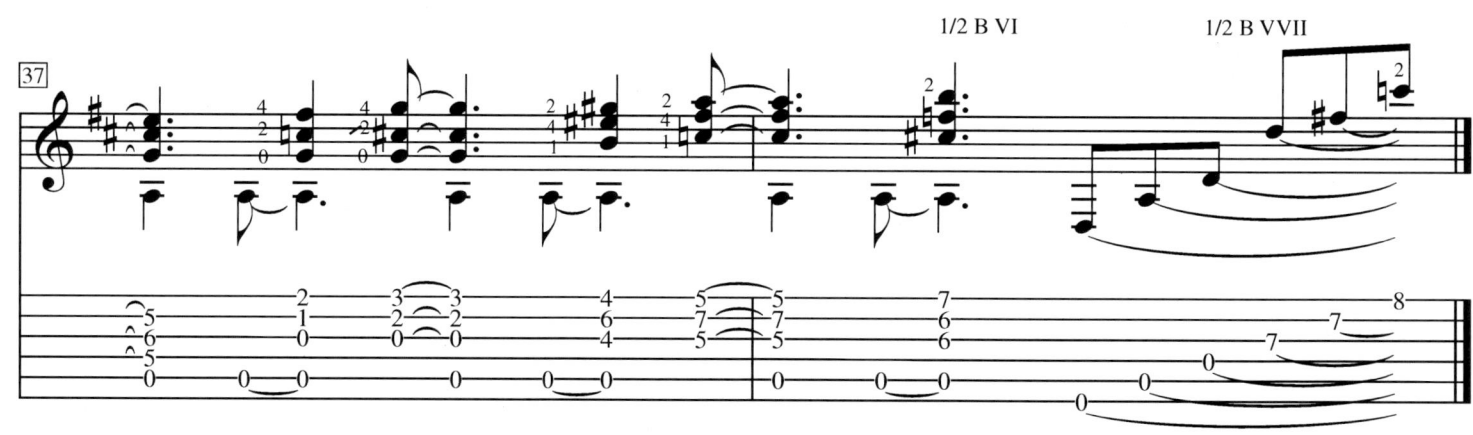

Cutback Blues
for Ed Hoad

William Beauvais

Track 4

Brisk, country swing
⑥=D ♩.=132

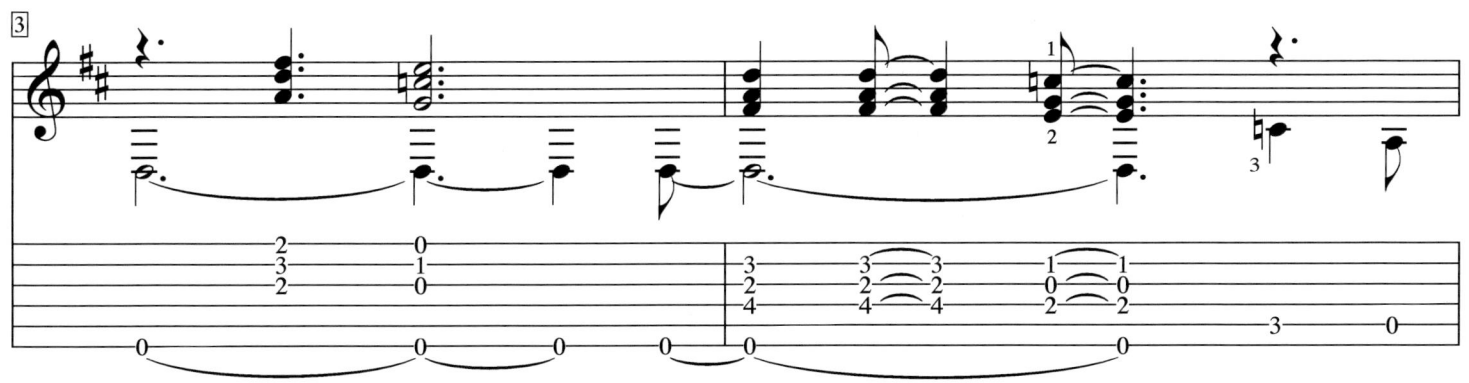

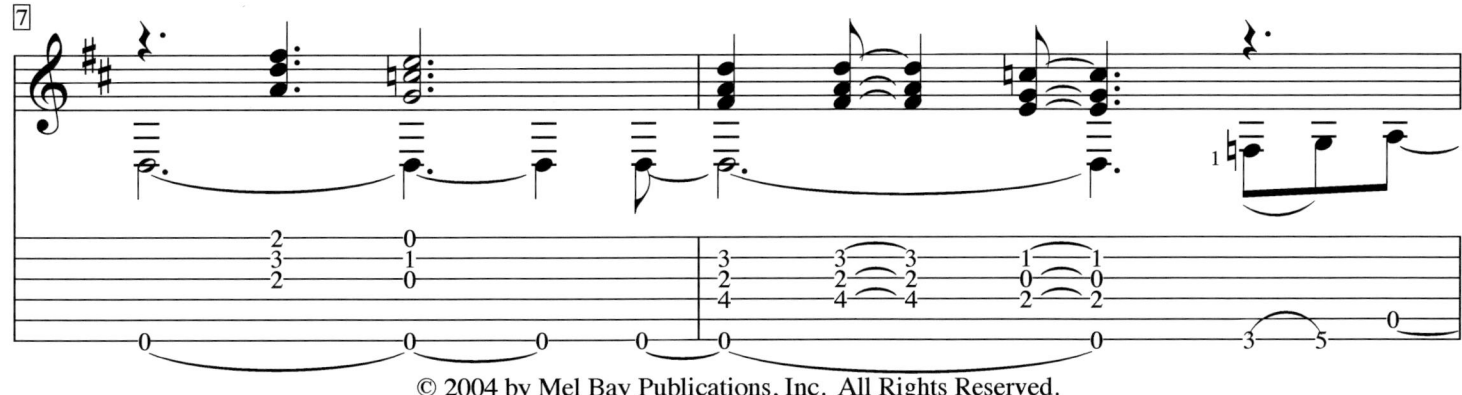

© 2004 by Mel Bay Publications, Inc. All Rights Reserved.

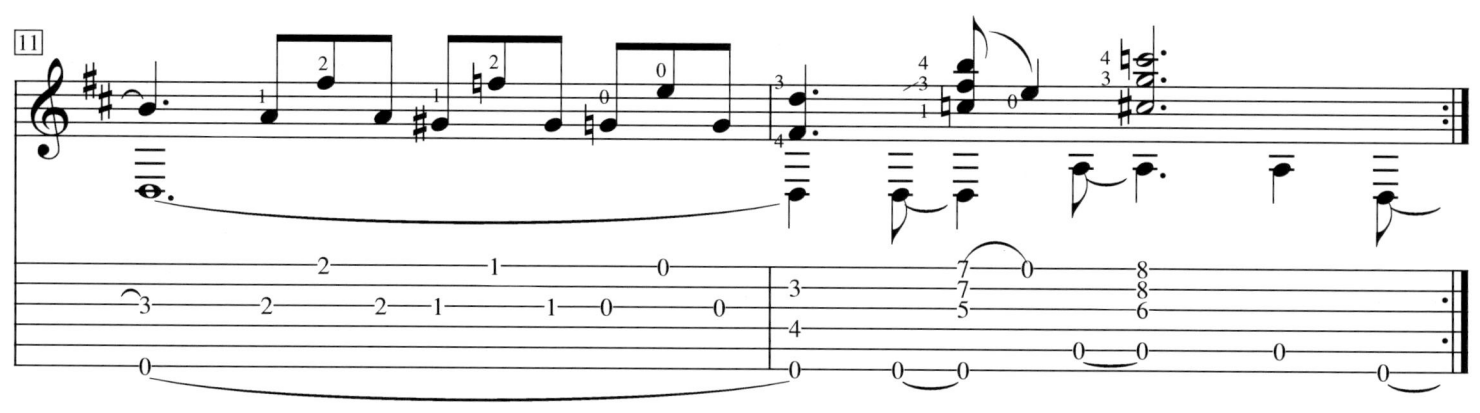

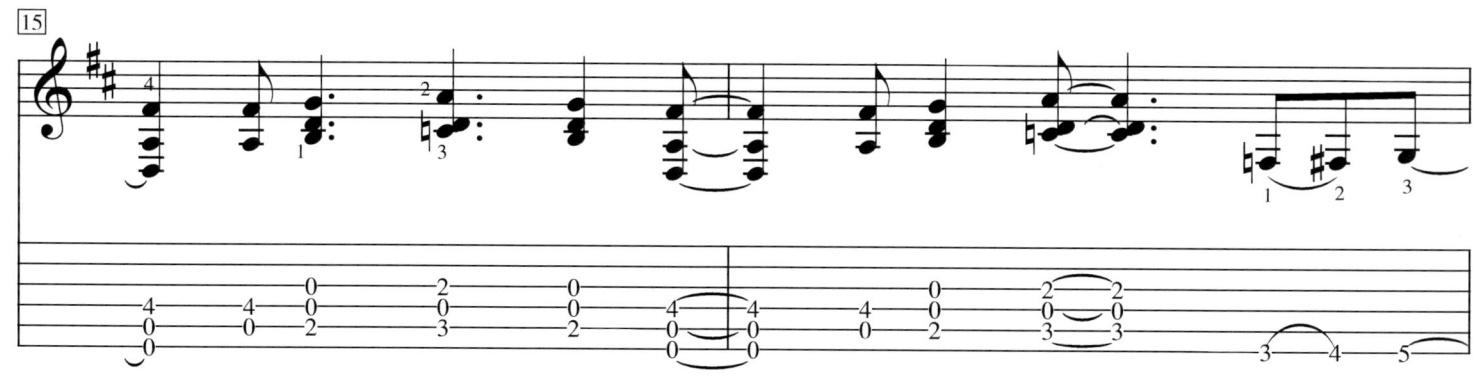

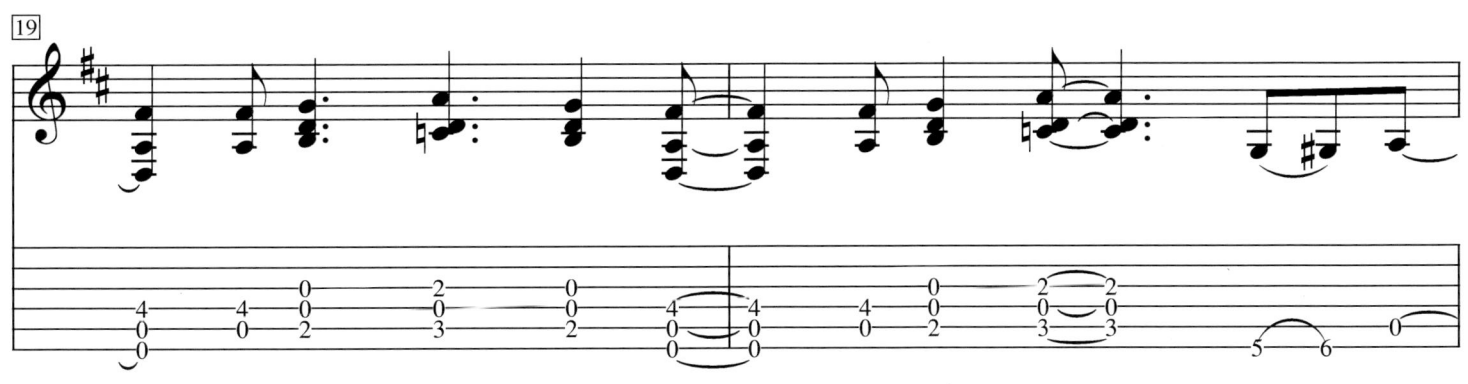
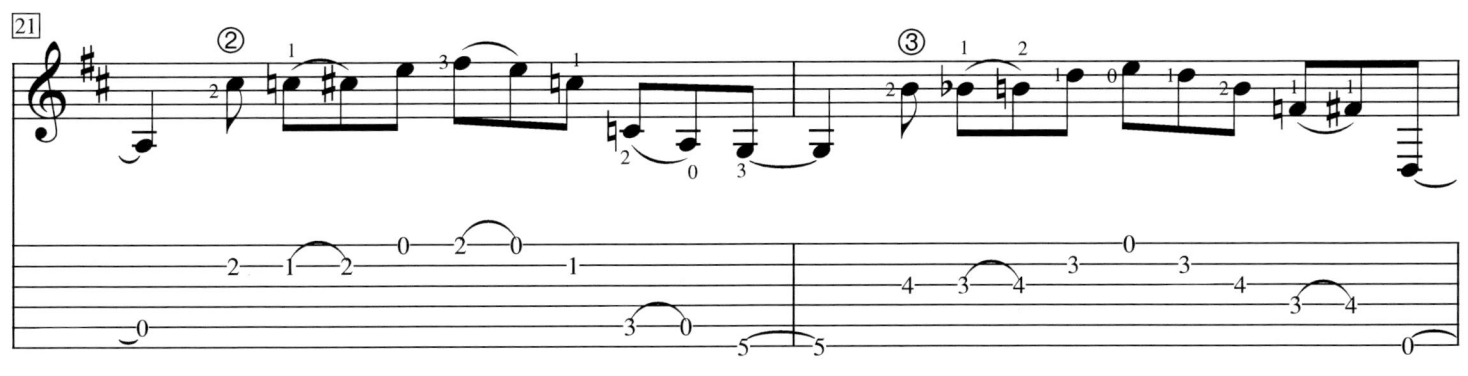

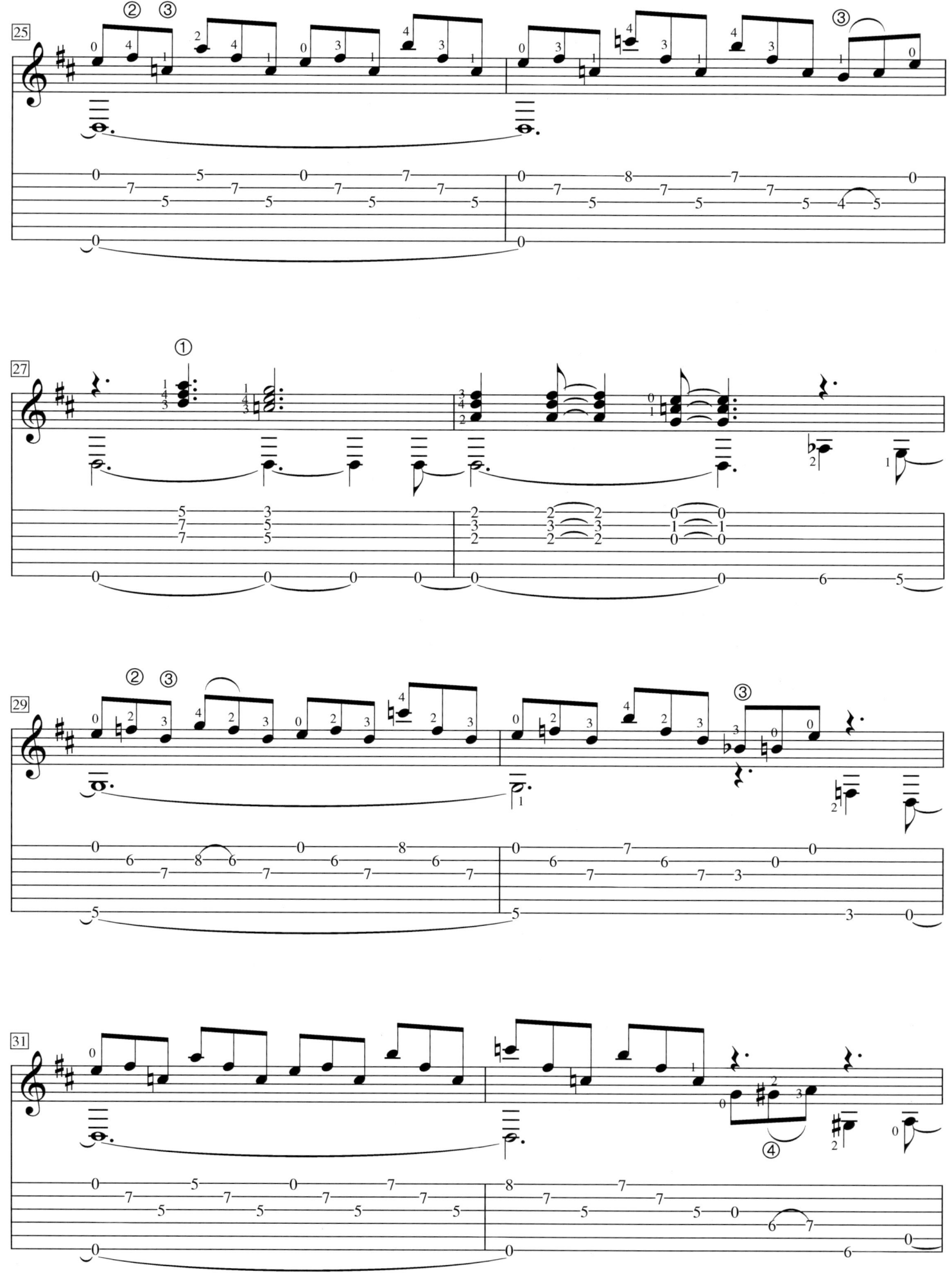

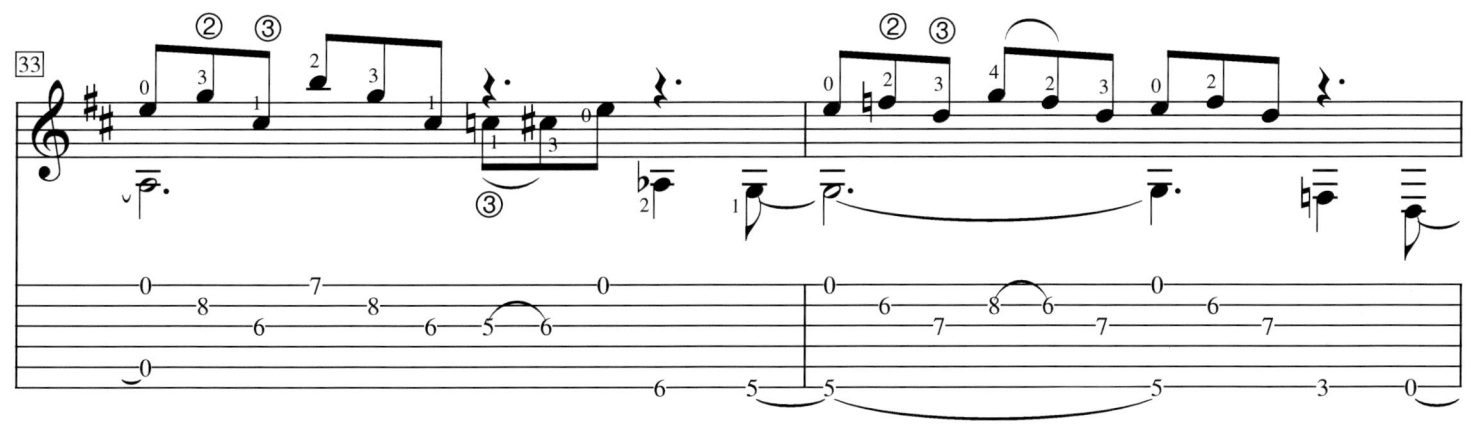

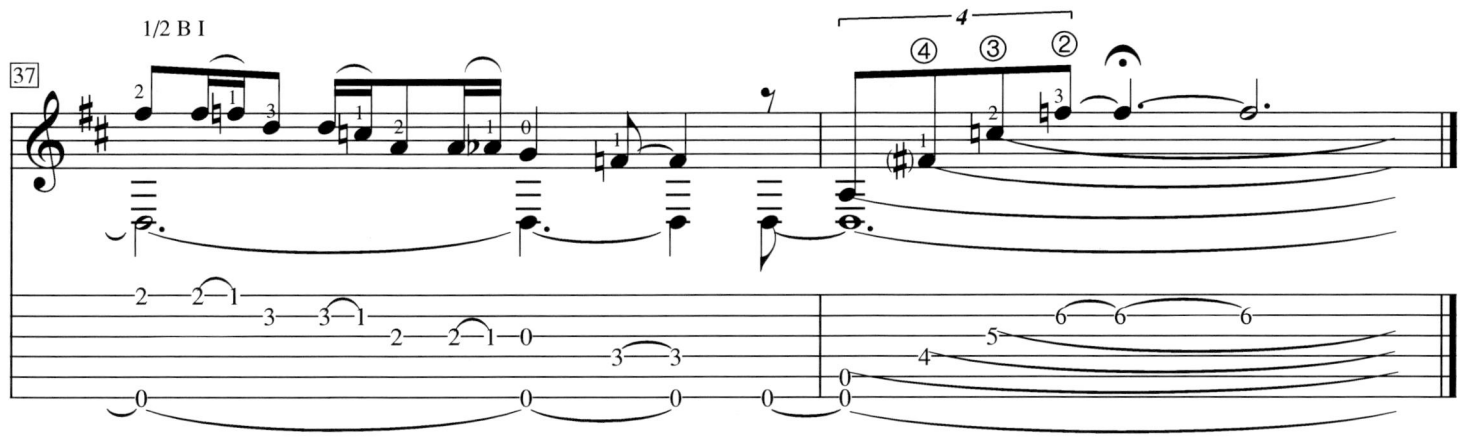

23

Gridlock Blues
for Ed Hoad

William Beauvais

Slowly, with feeling
♩.=56

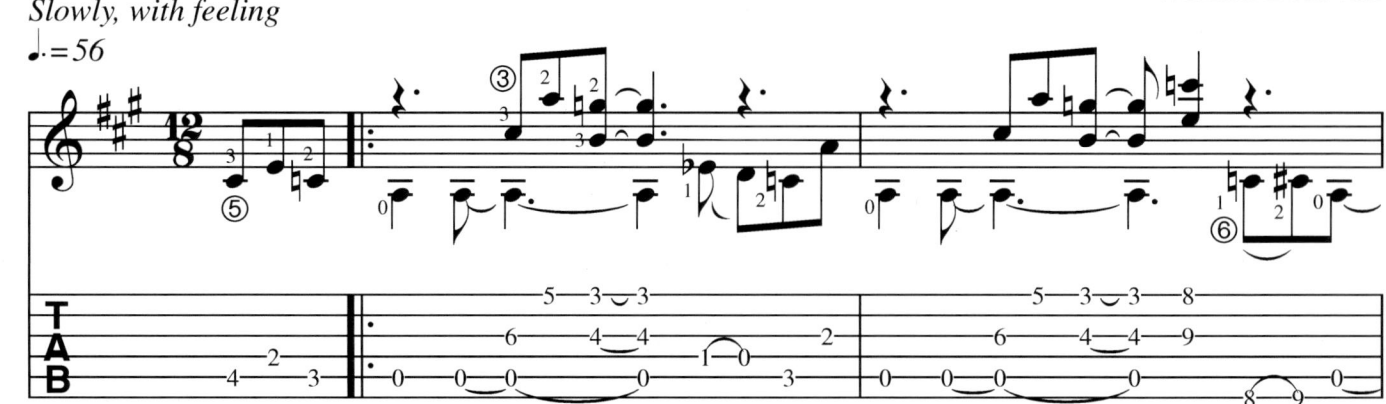
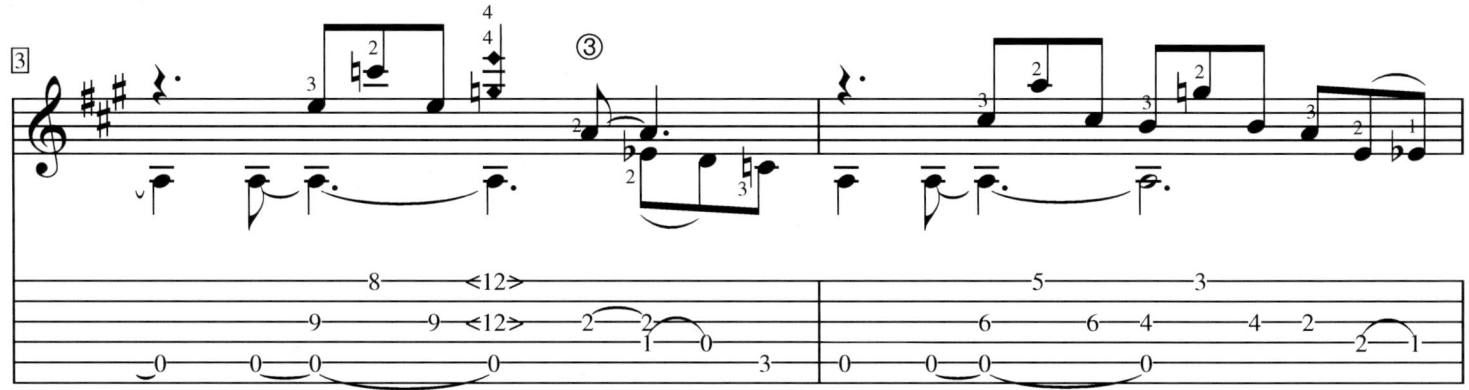
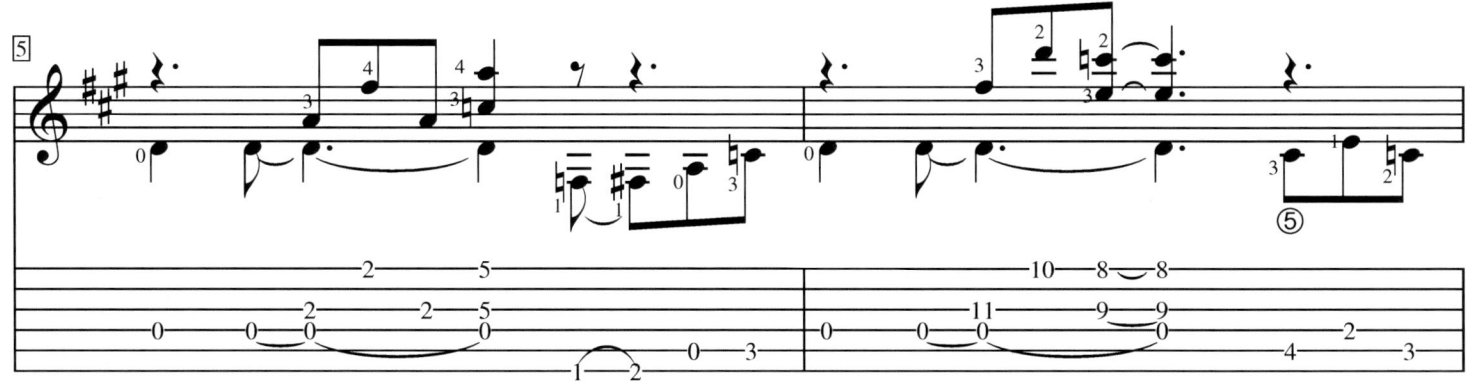
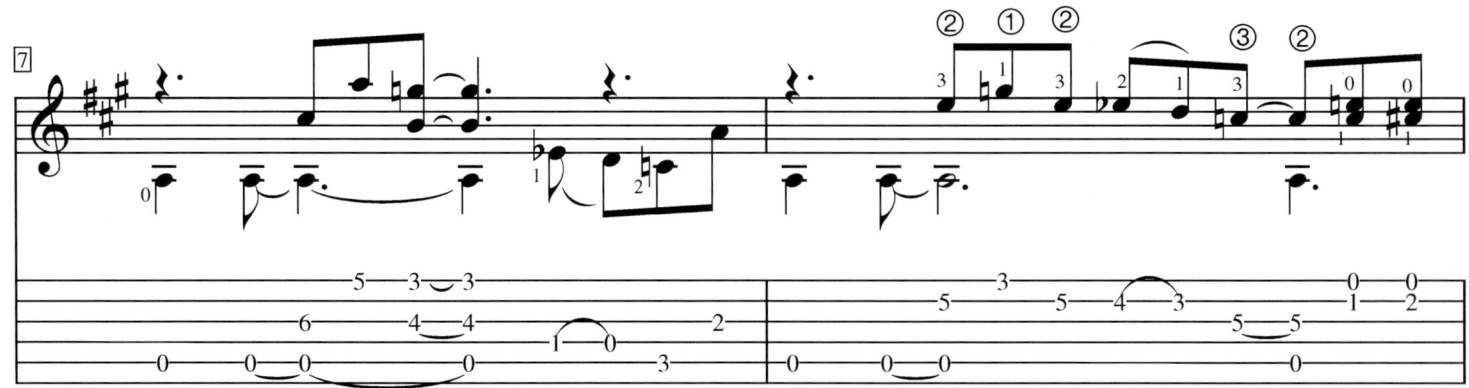

© 2004 by Mel Bay Publications, Inc. All Rights Reserved.

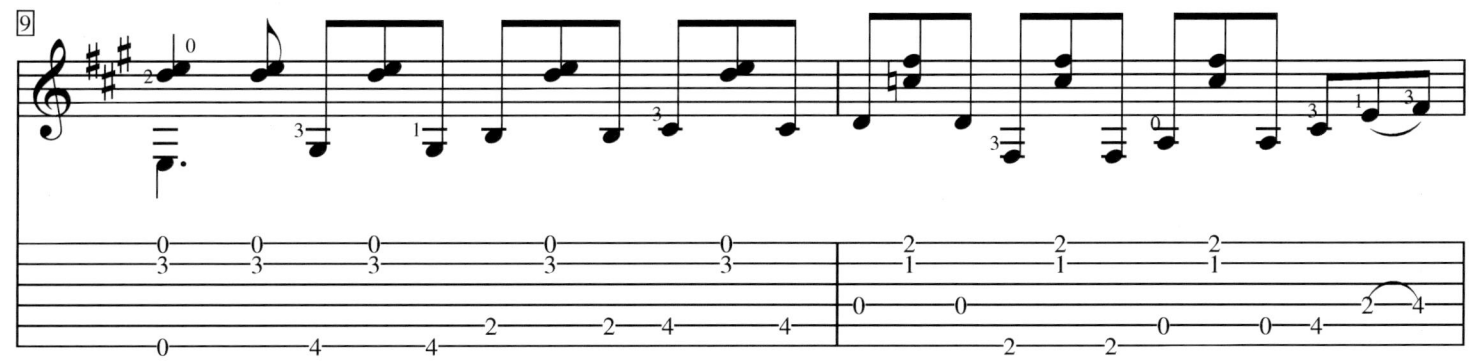
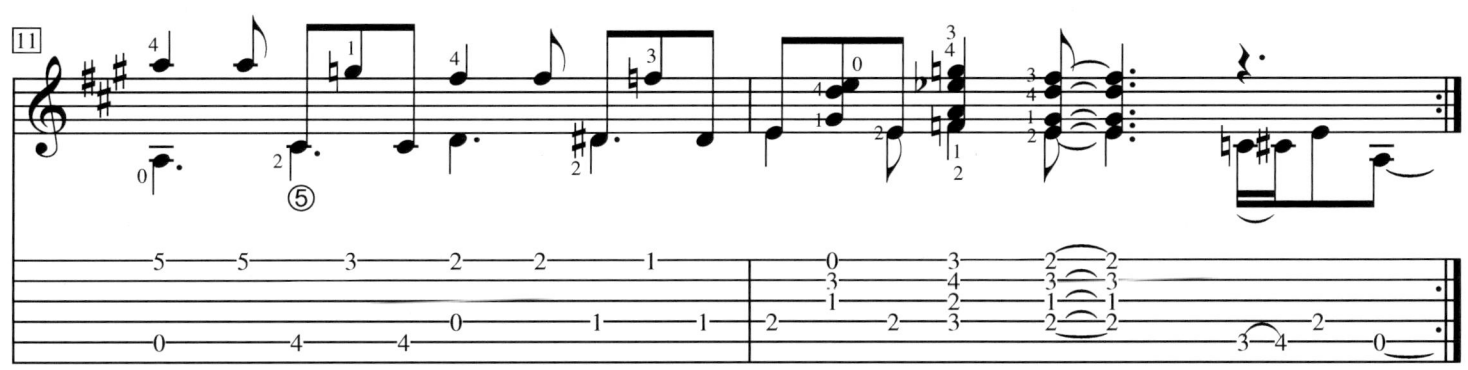
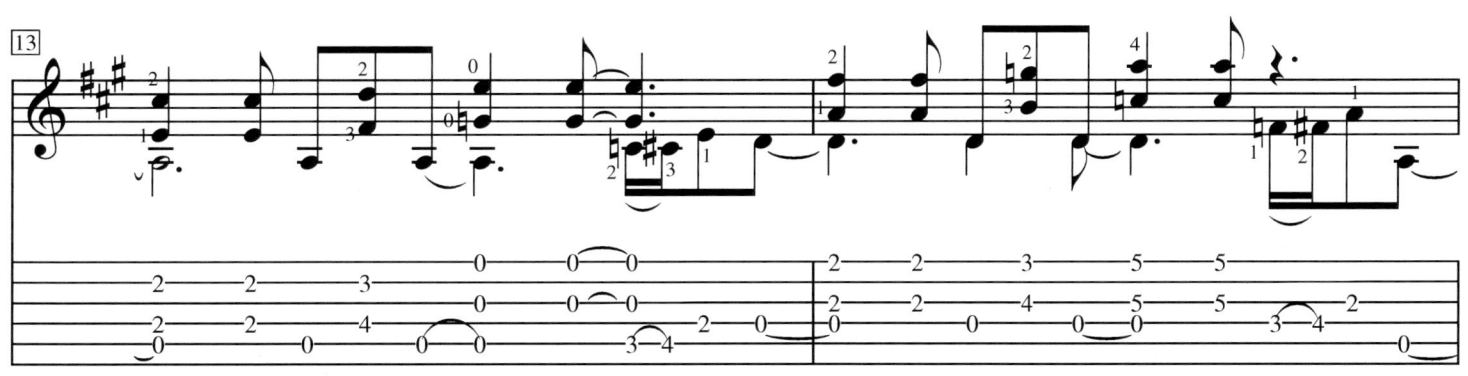

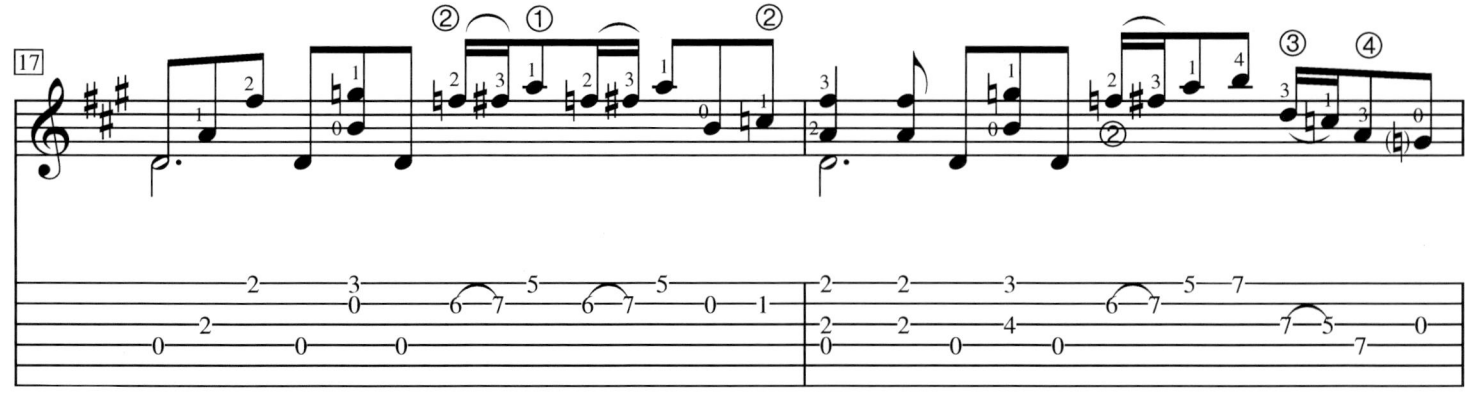
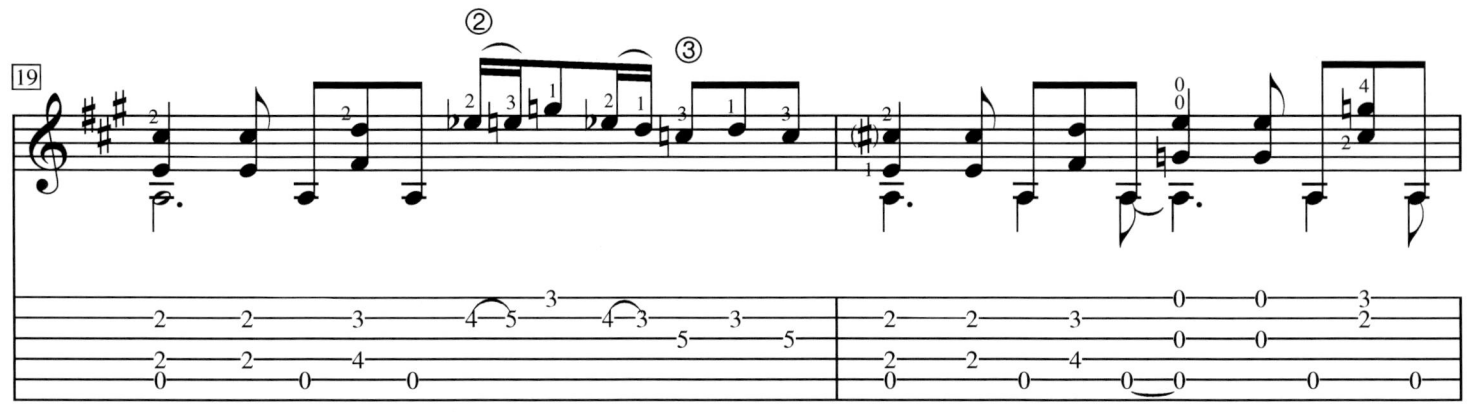
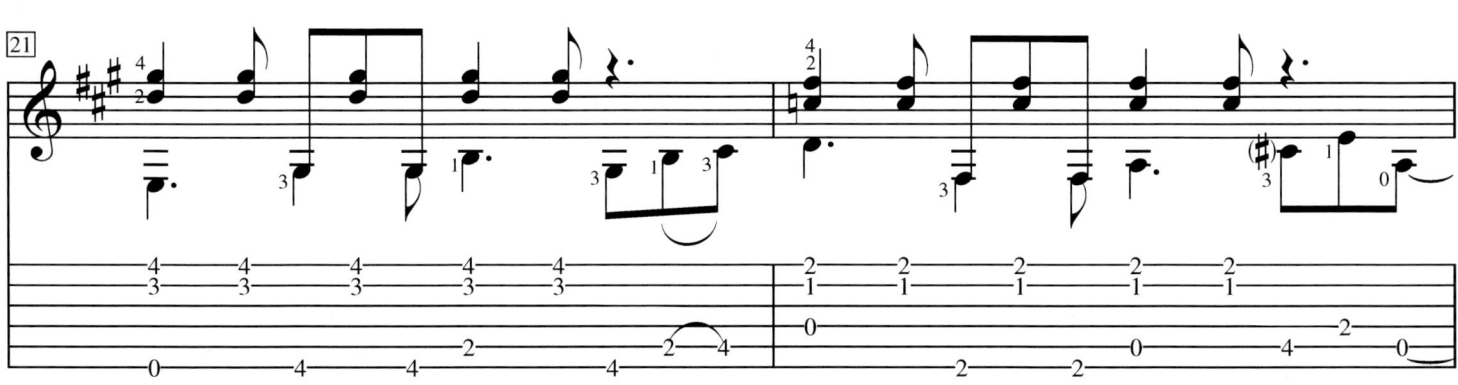
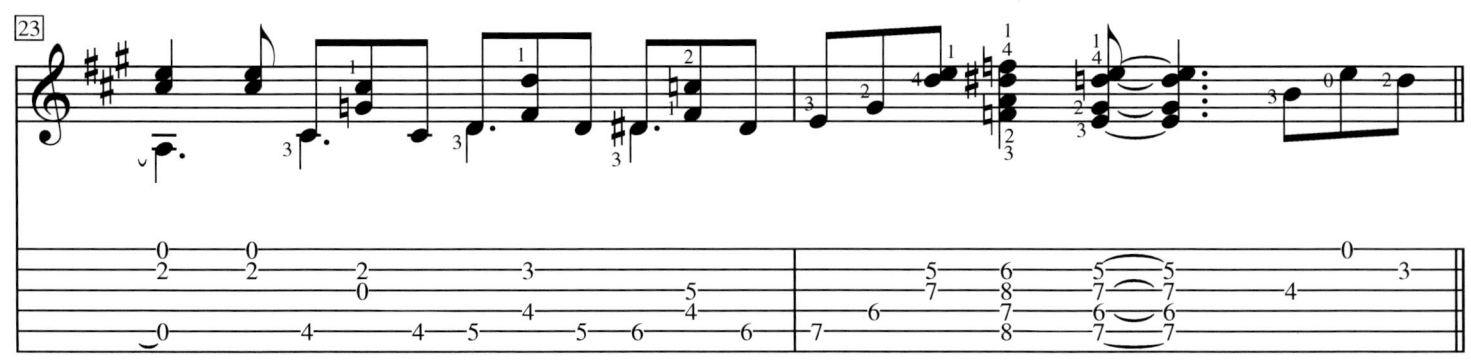

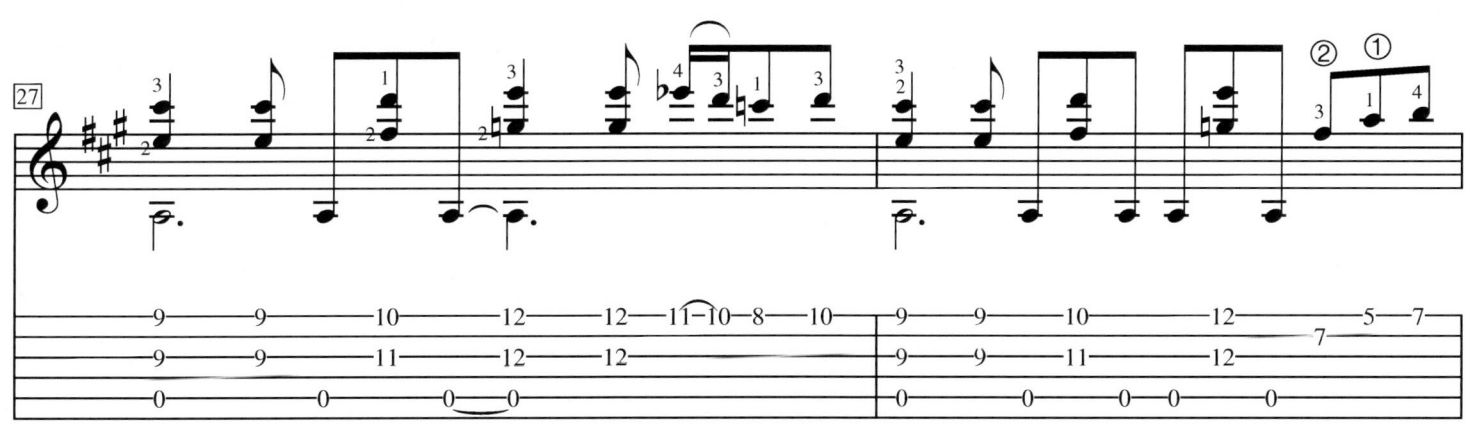
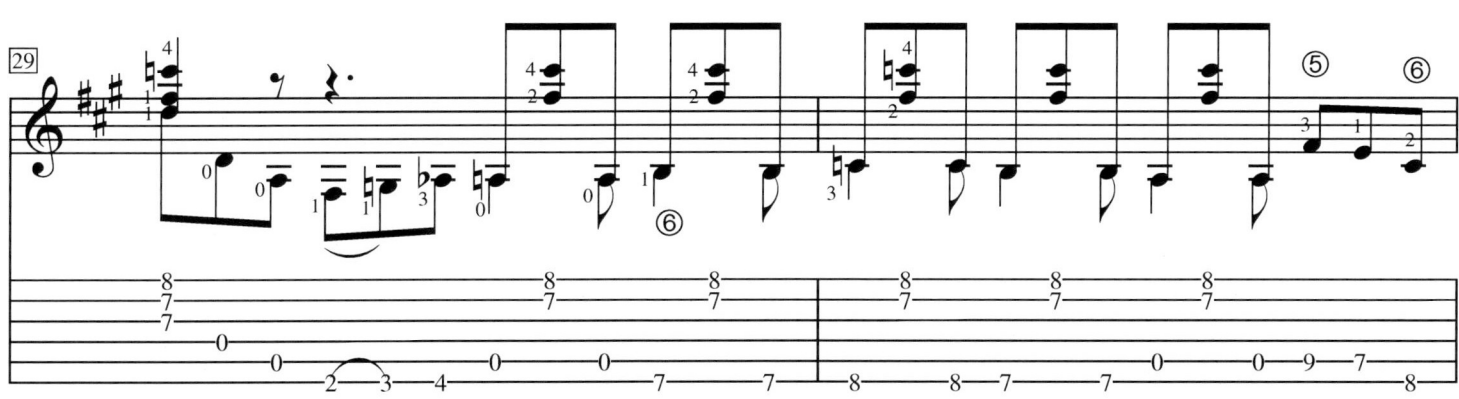
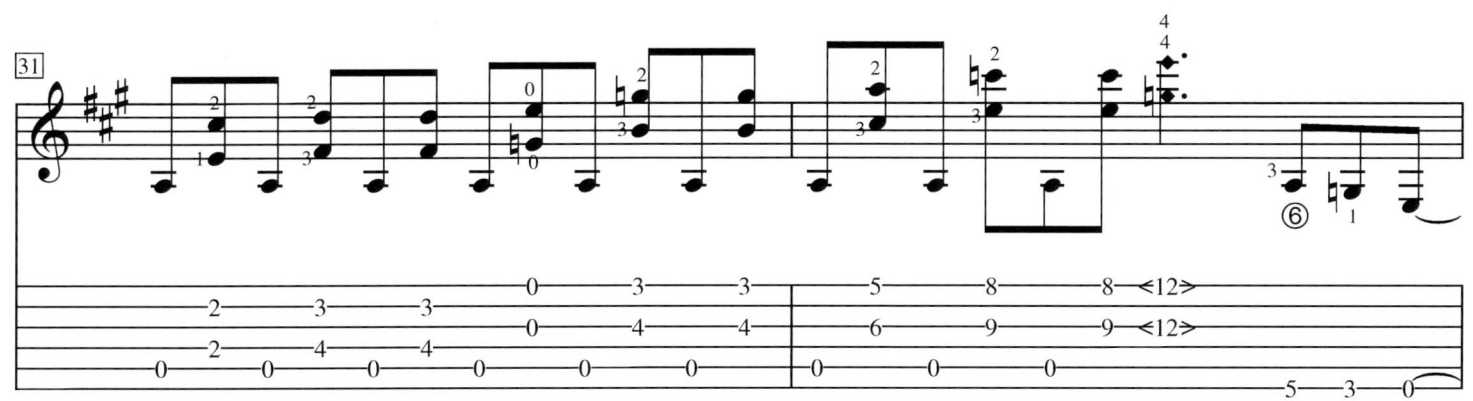

This page has been left blank to avoid awkward page turns.

Rainy Weekend Blues
for Peter Hudson

William Beauvais

Brisk, country swing
♩. = 140

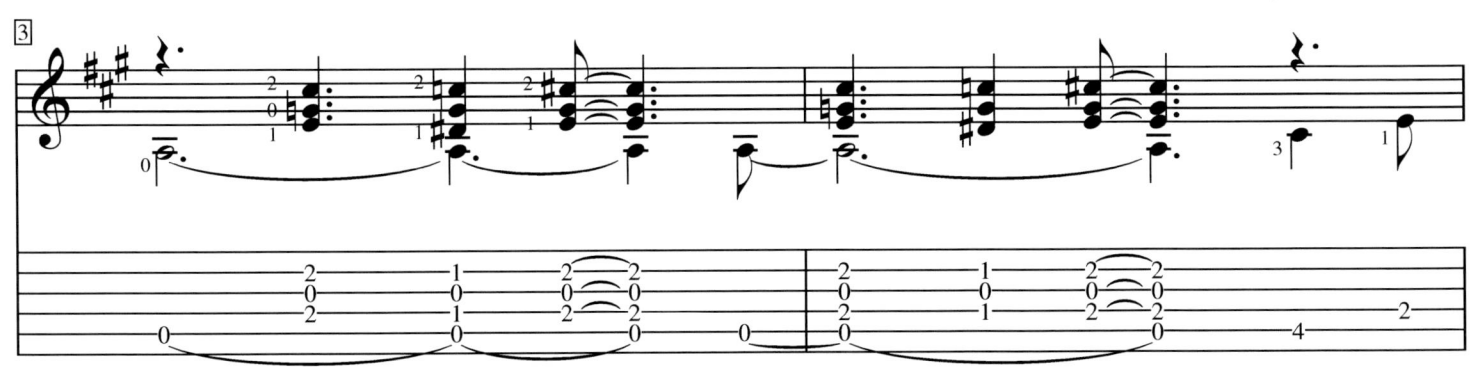

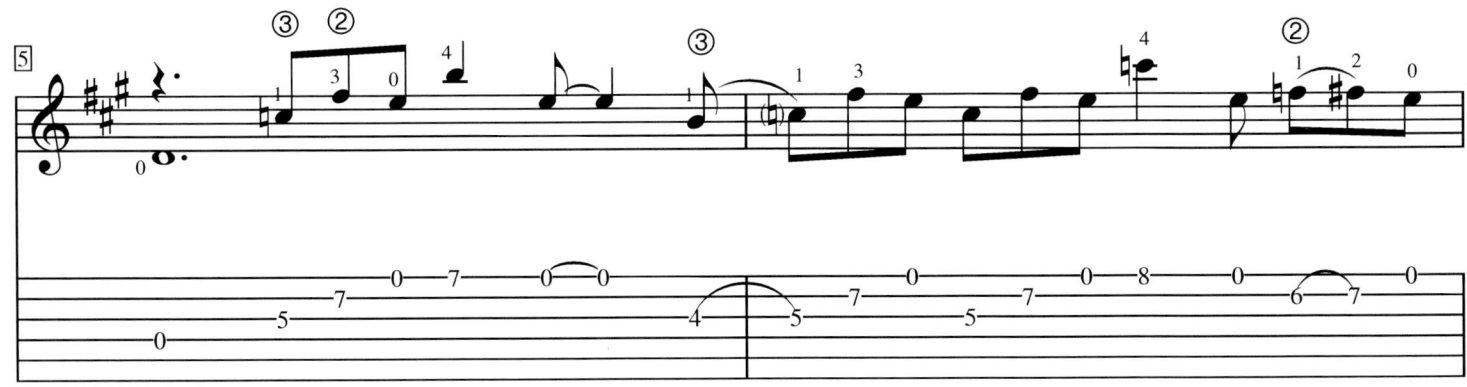

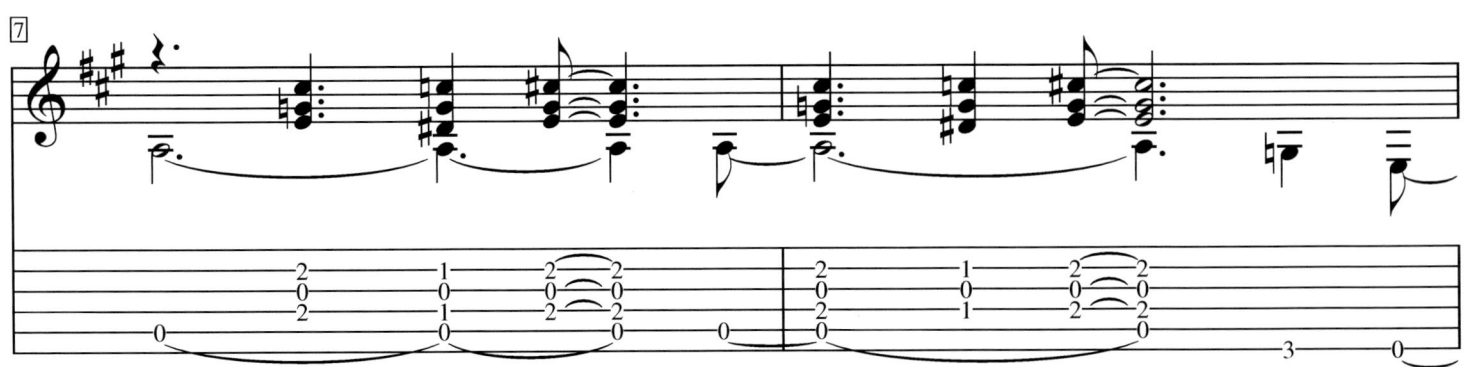

© 2004 by Mel Bay Publications, Inc. All Rights Reserved.

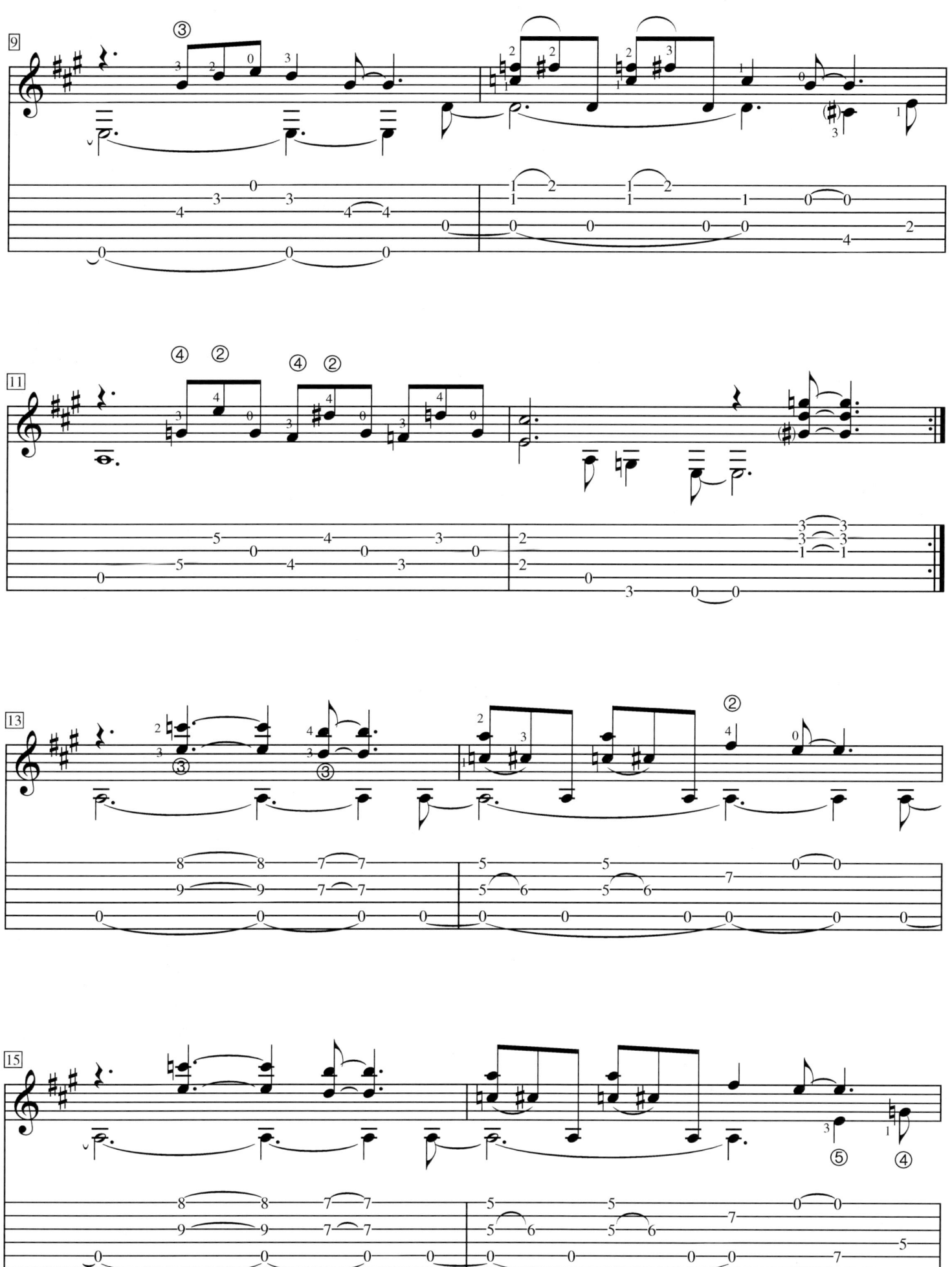

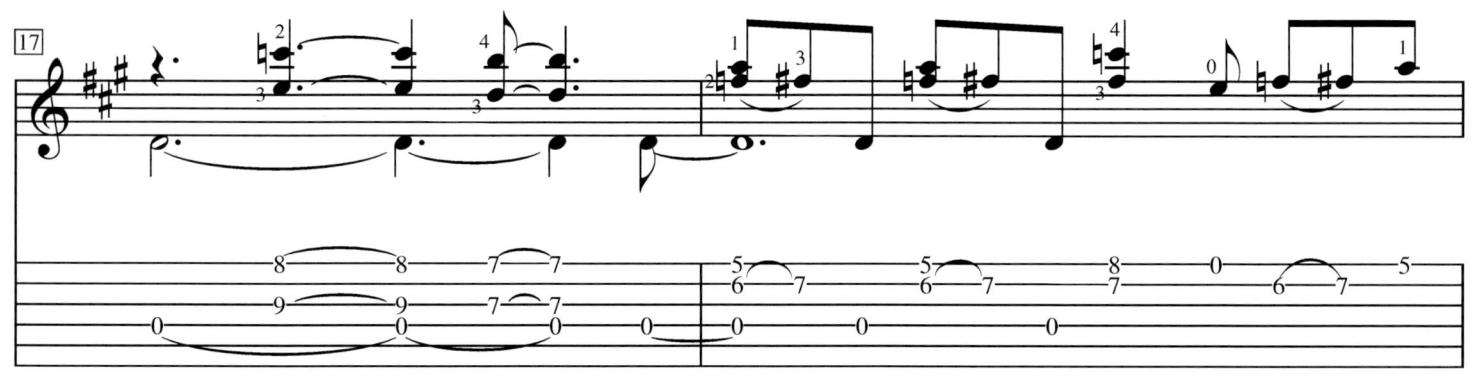
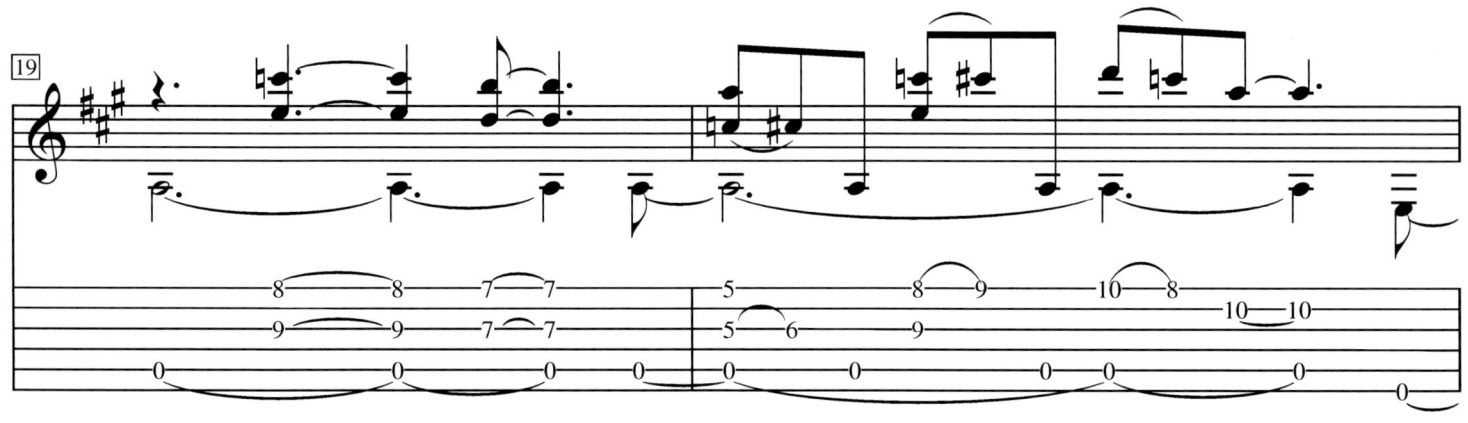
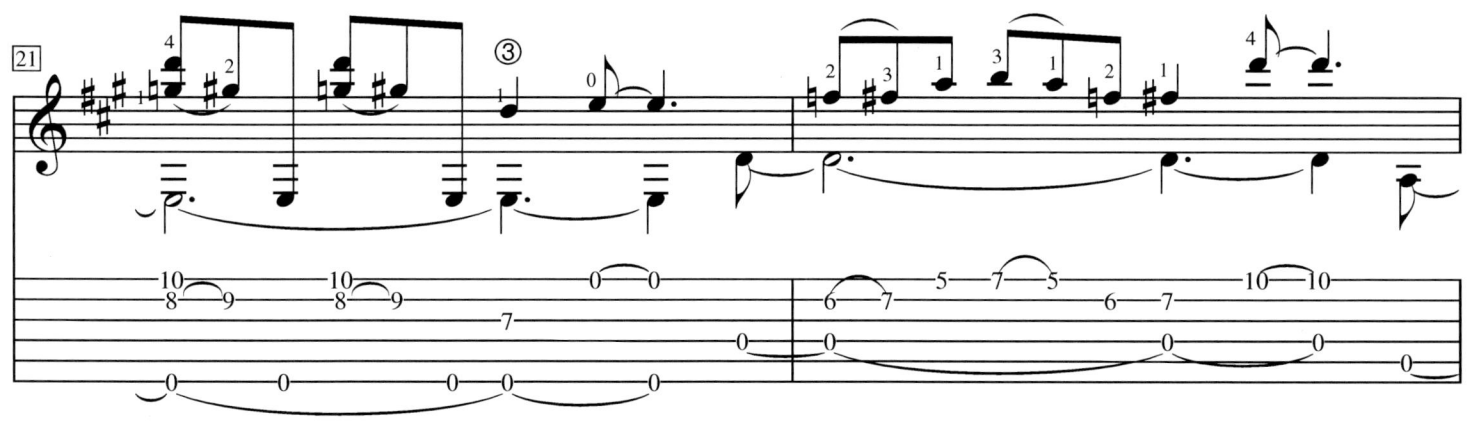
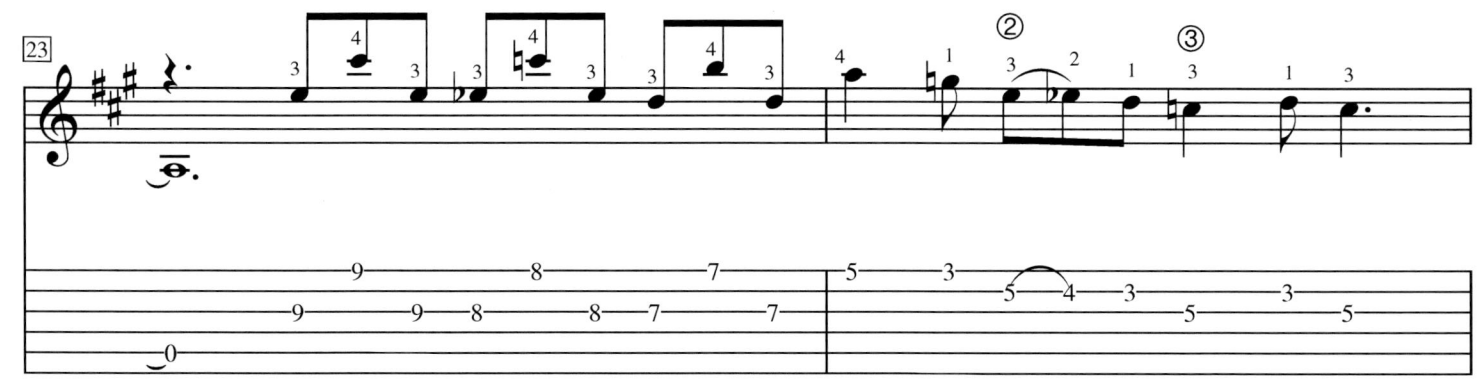

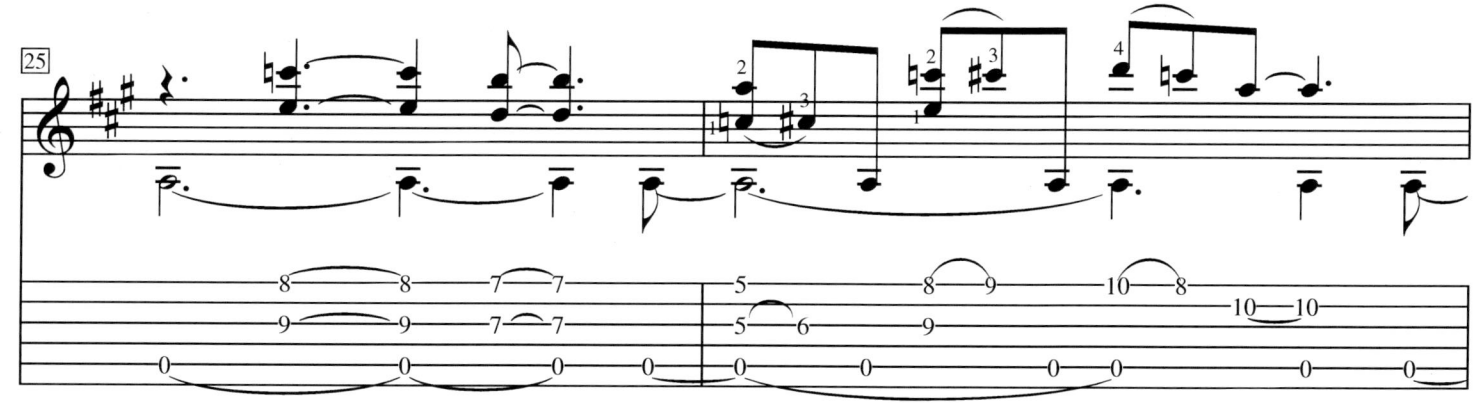
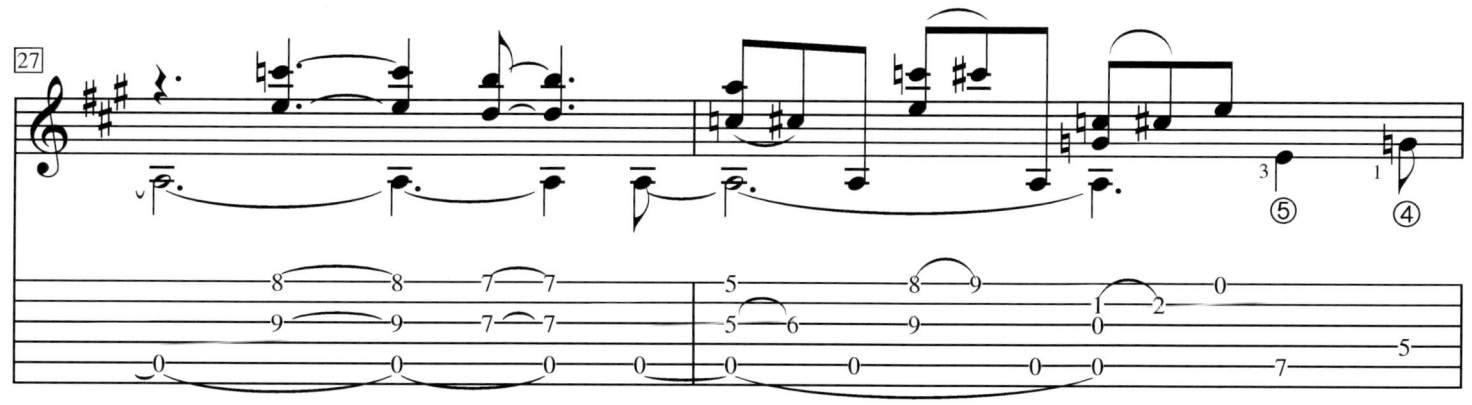
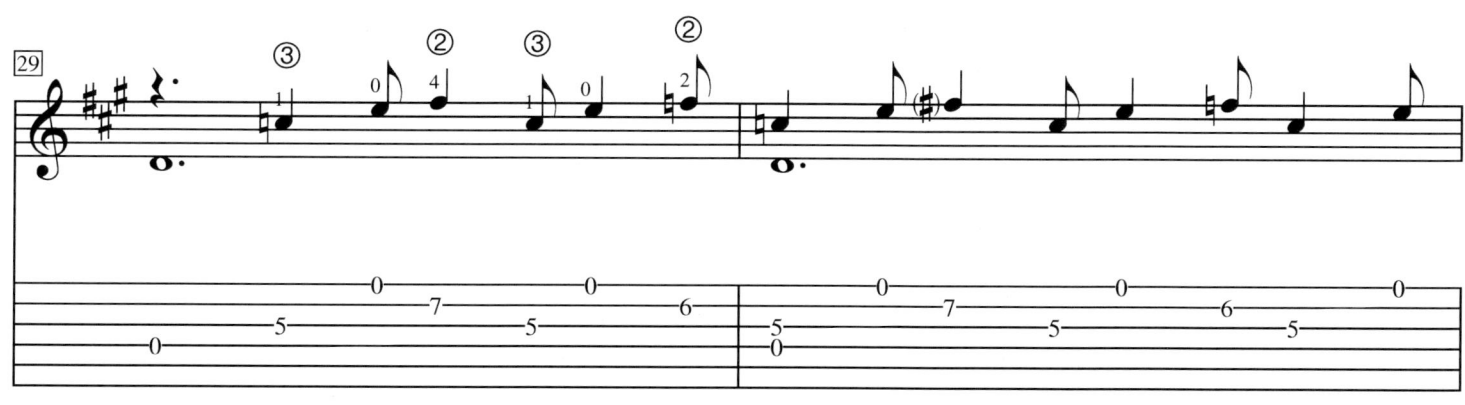

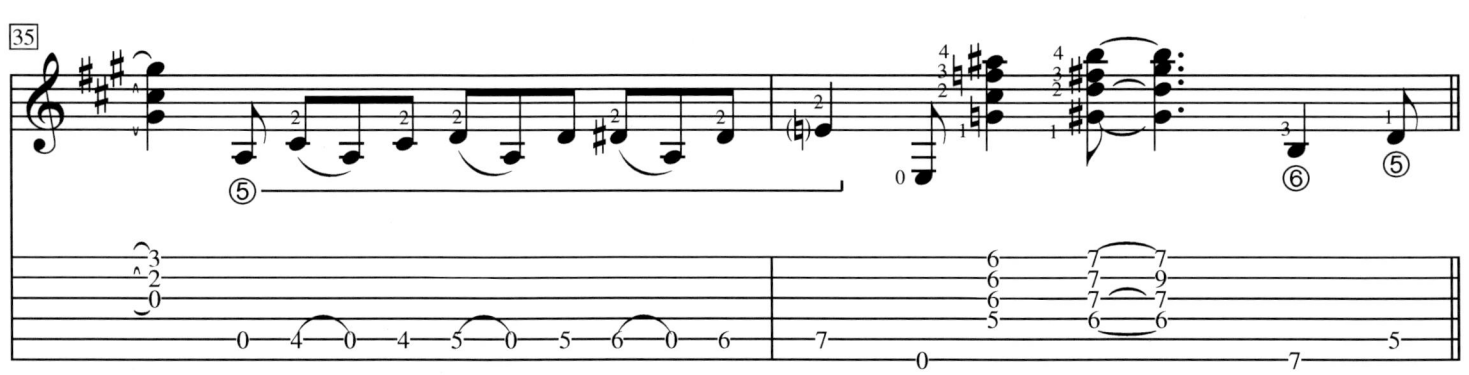

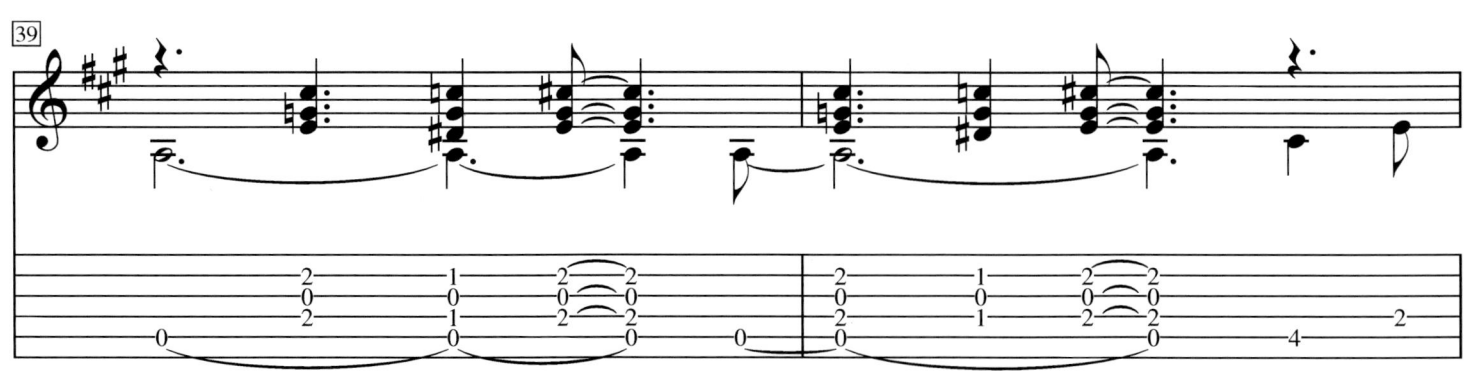

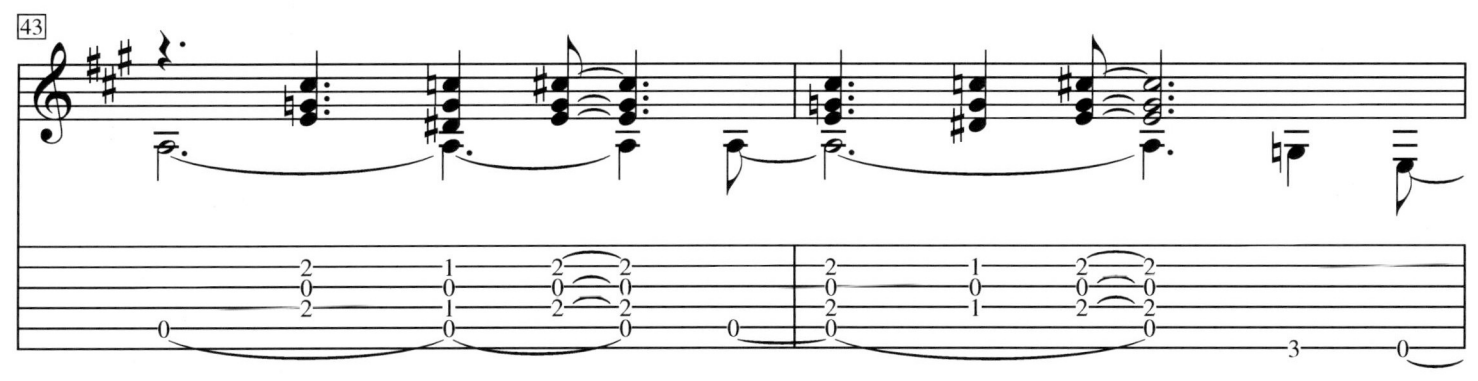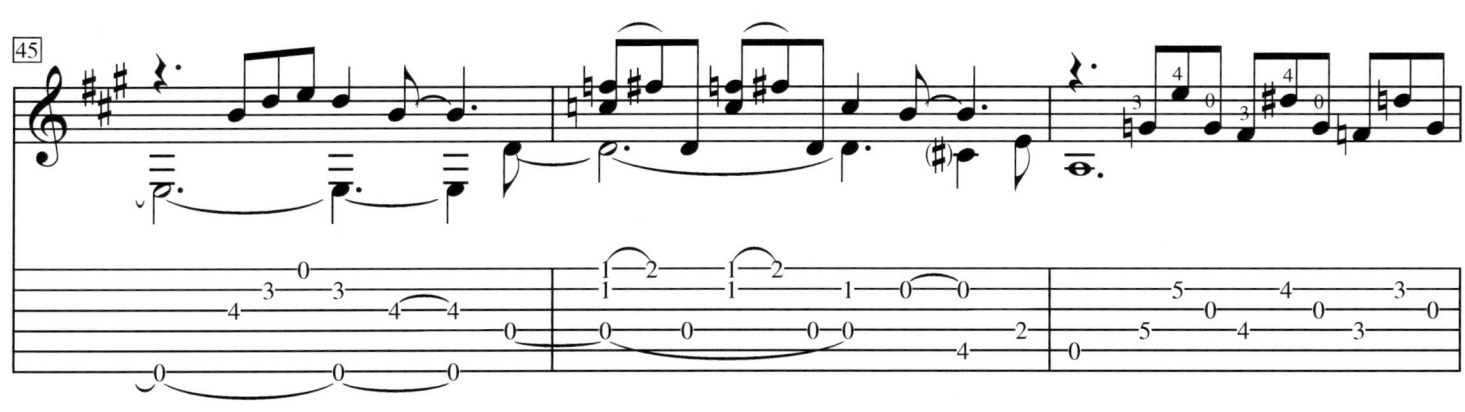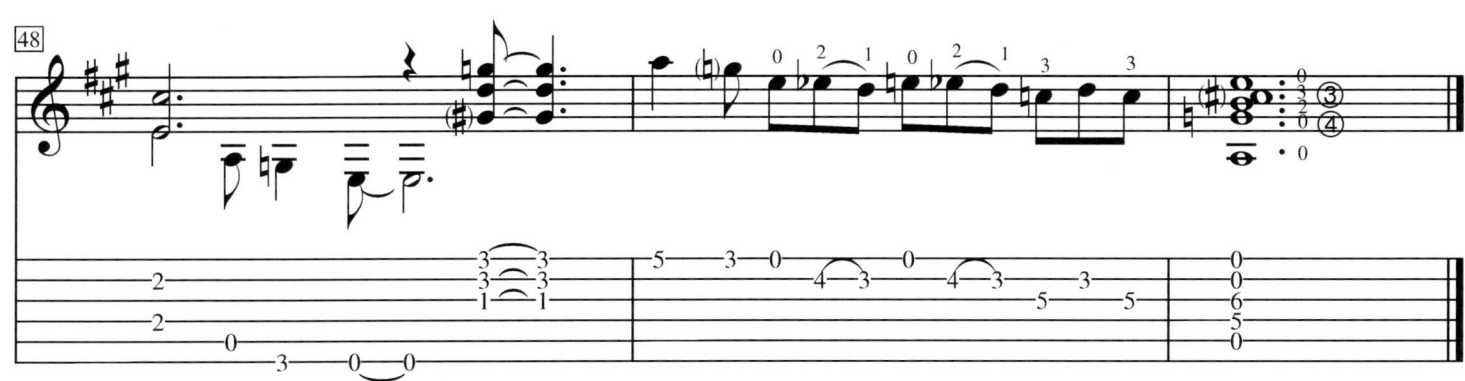

Snaky Blue Line
for Peter Hudson

William Beauvais

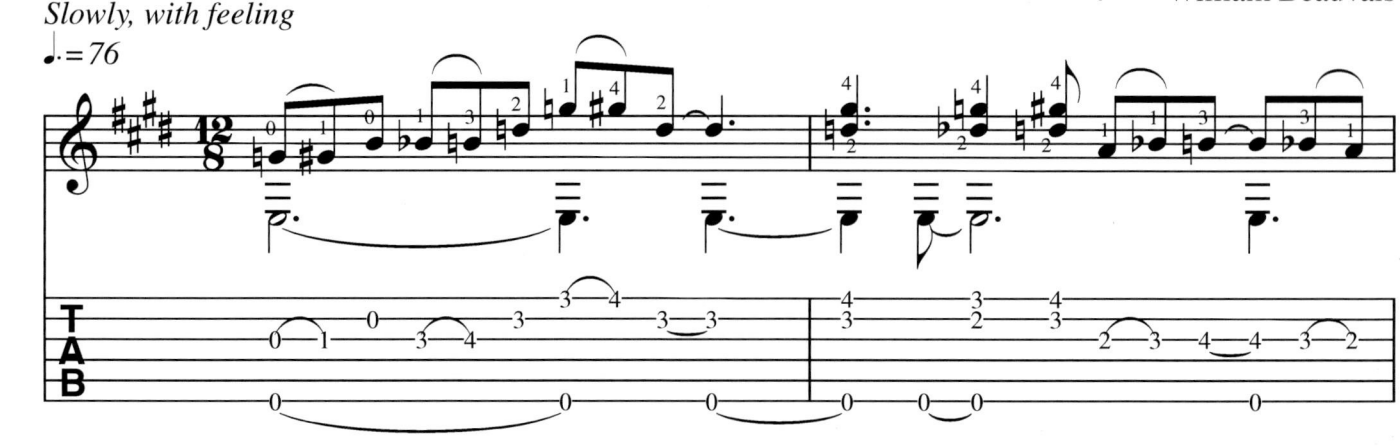
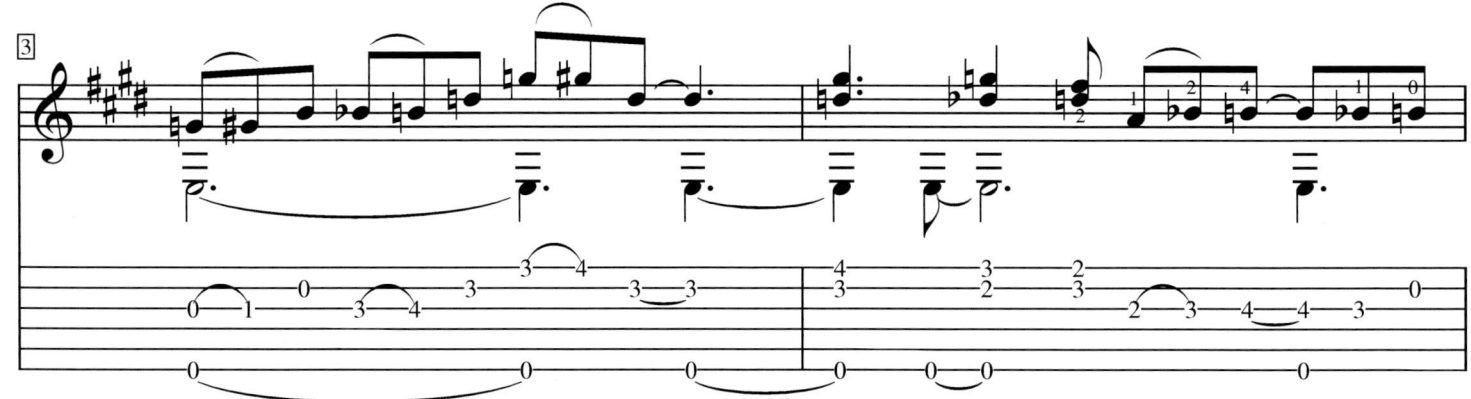
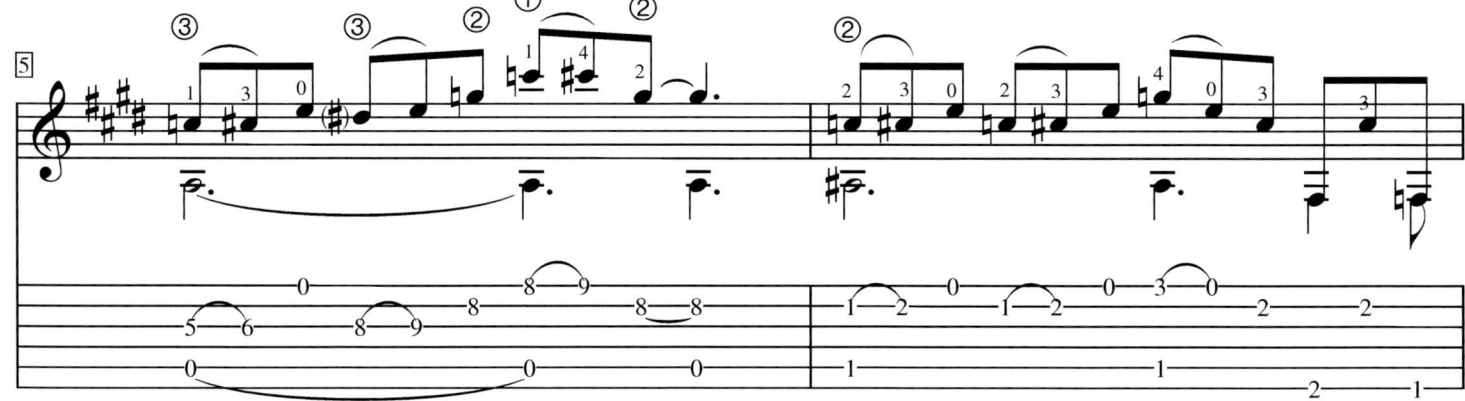

© 2004 by Mel Bay Publications, Inc. All Rights Reserved.

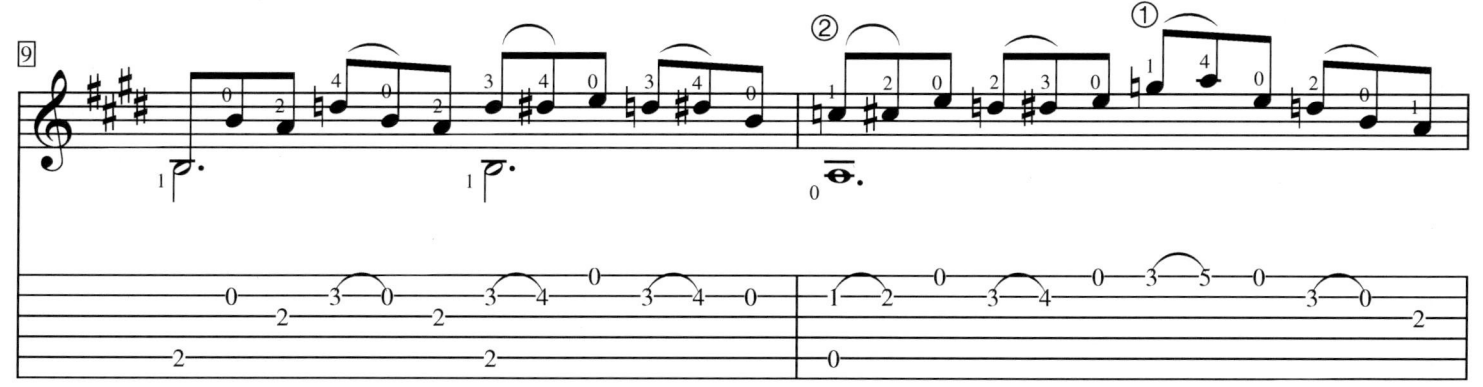
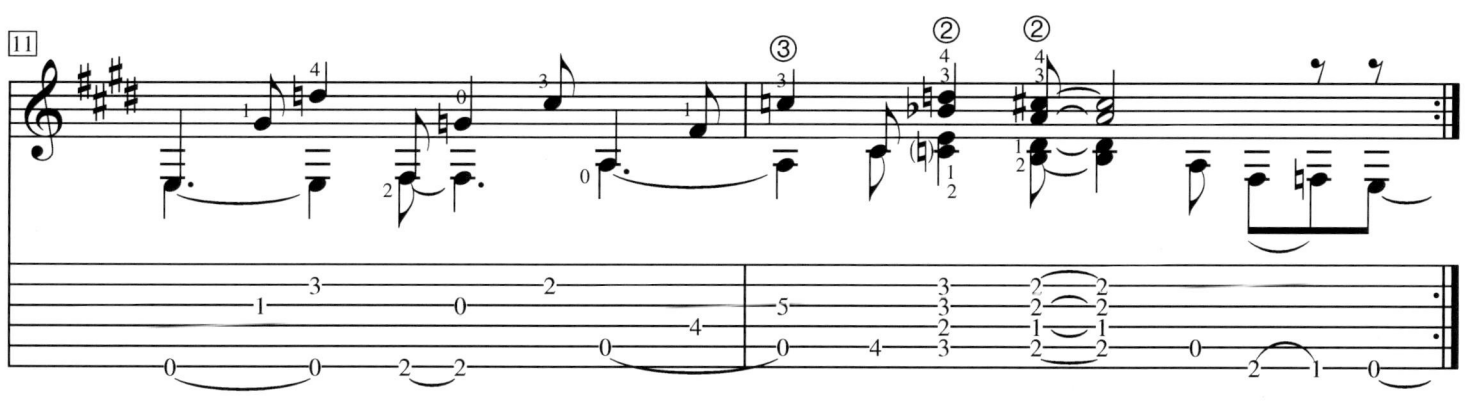
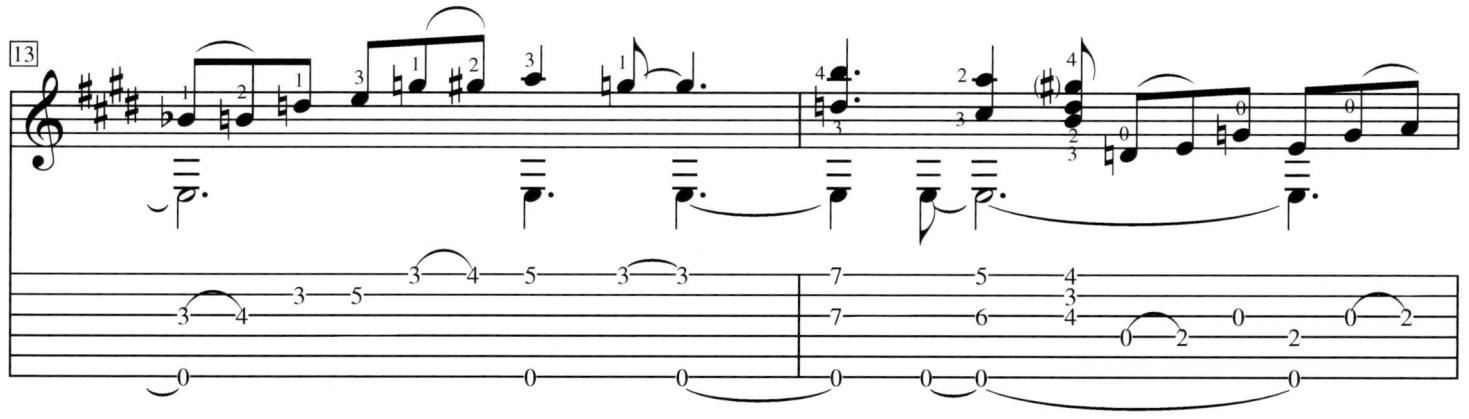
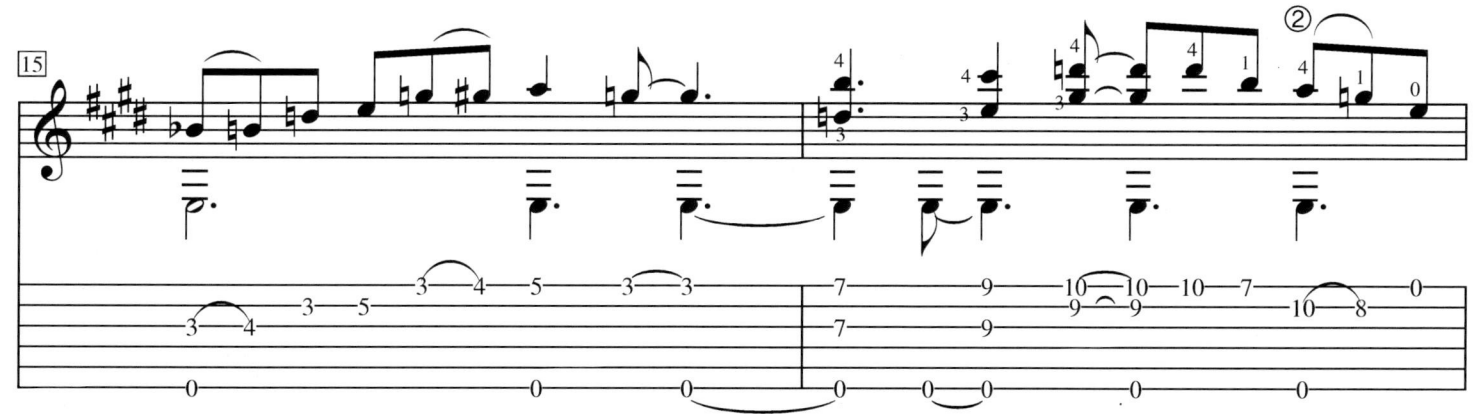

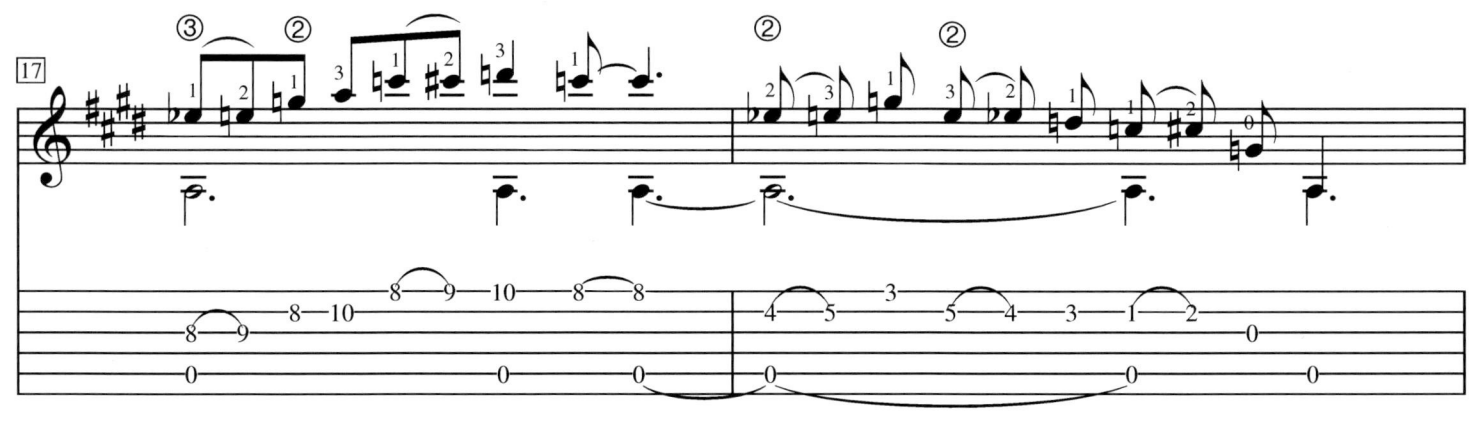
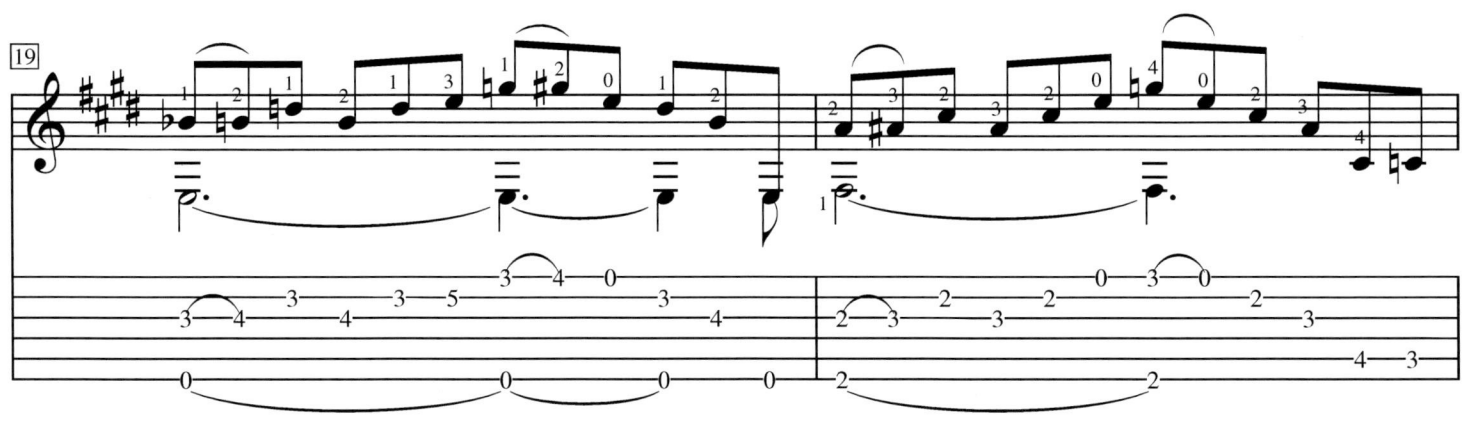
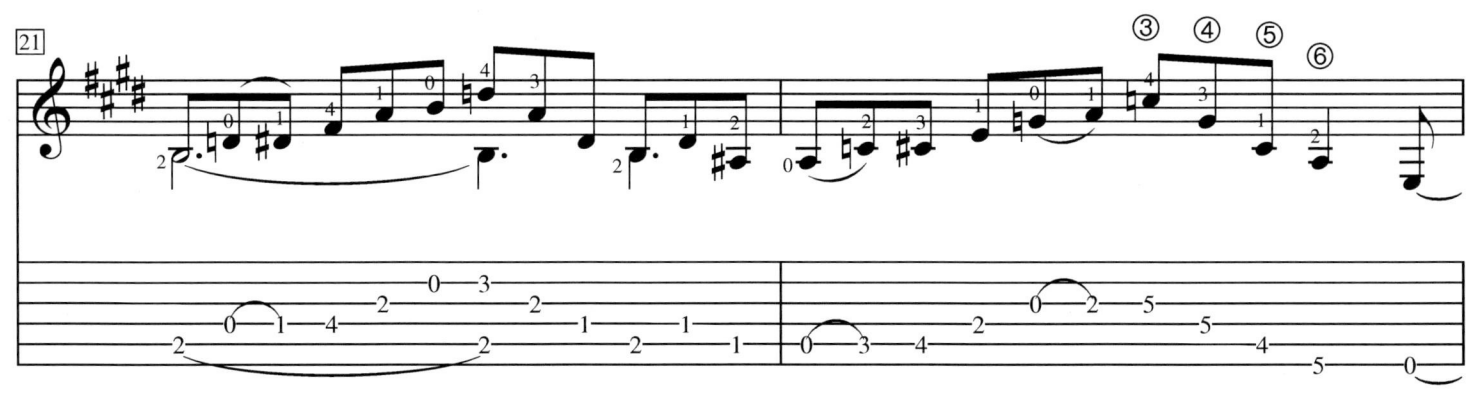

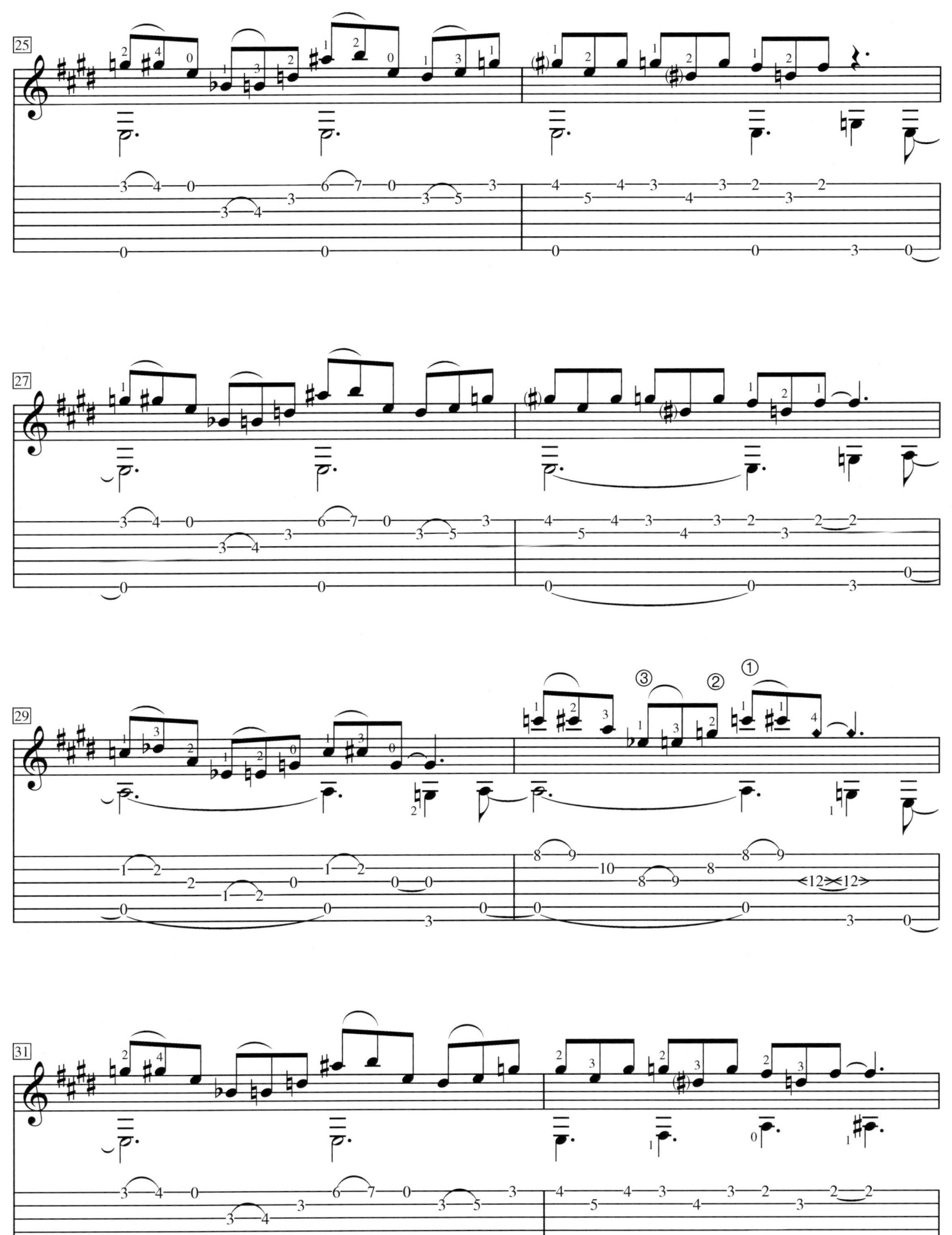

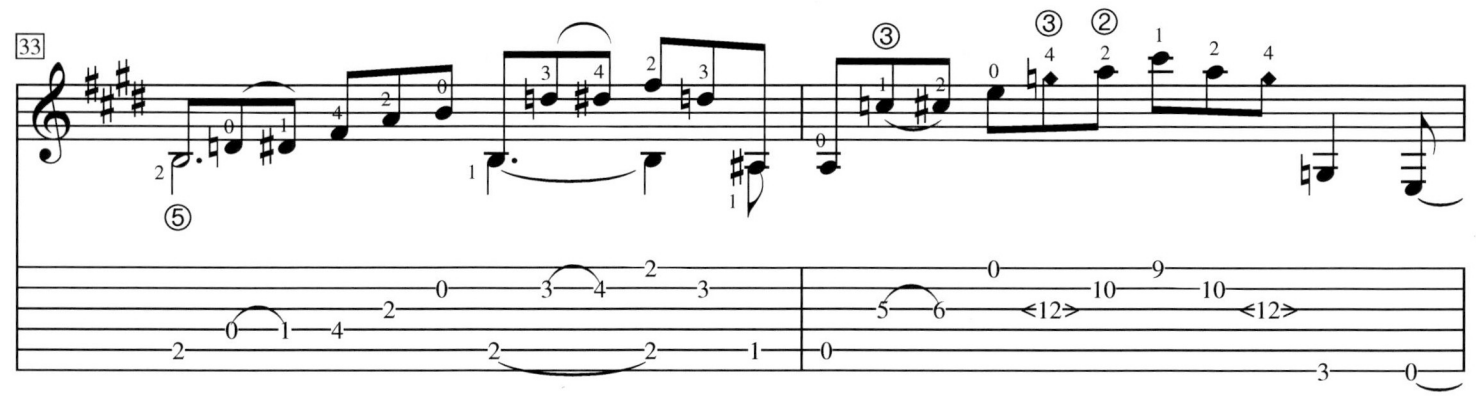
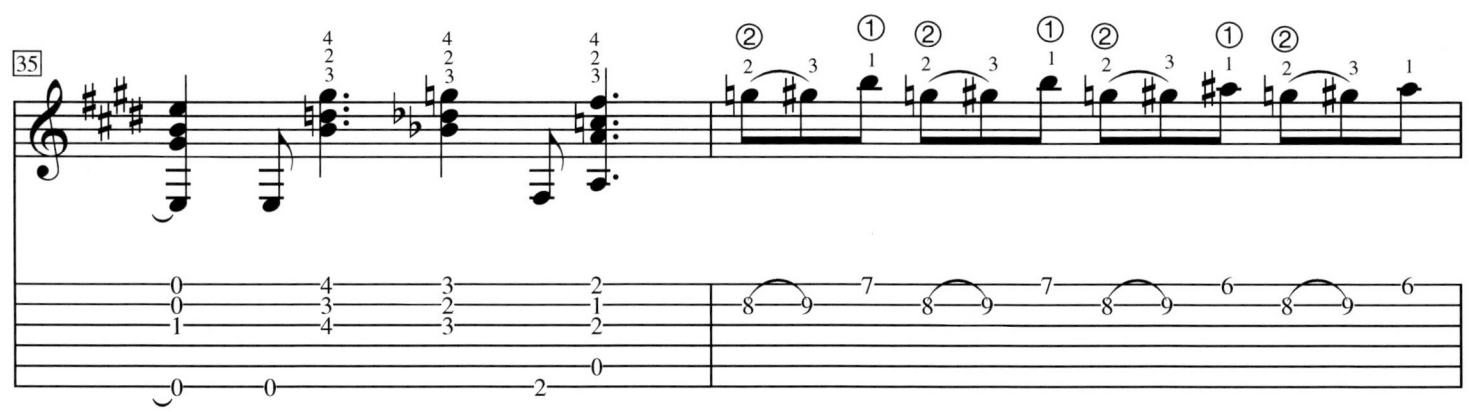
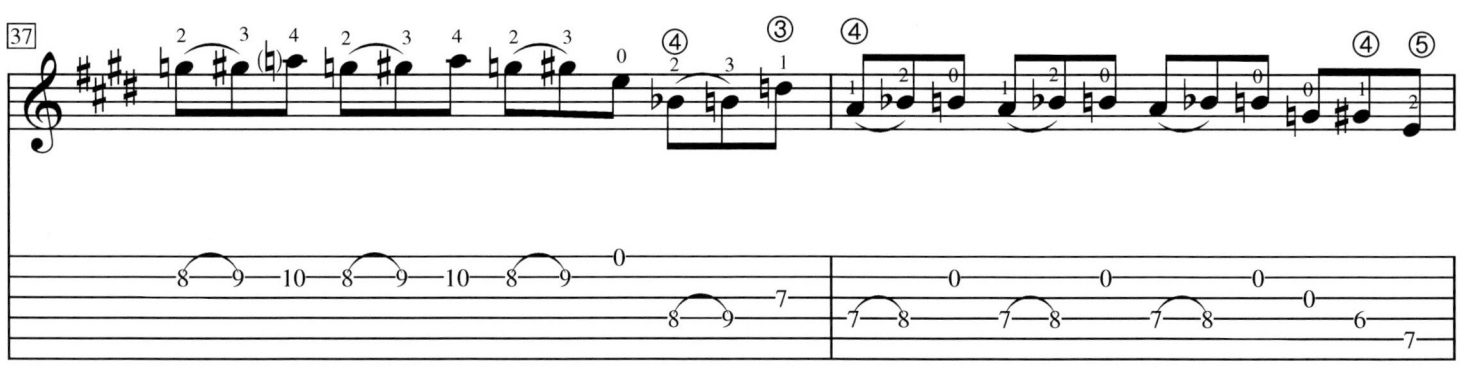

Chicago Style Blues
for Gary Gontier

William Beauvais

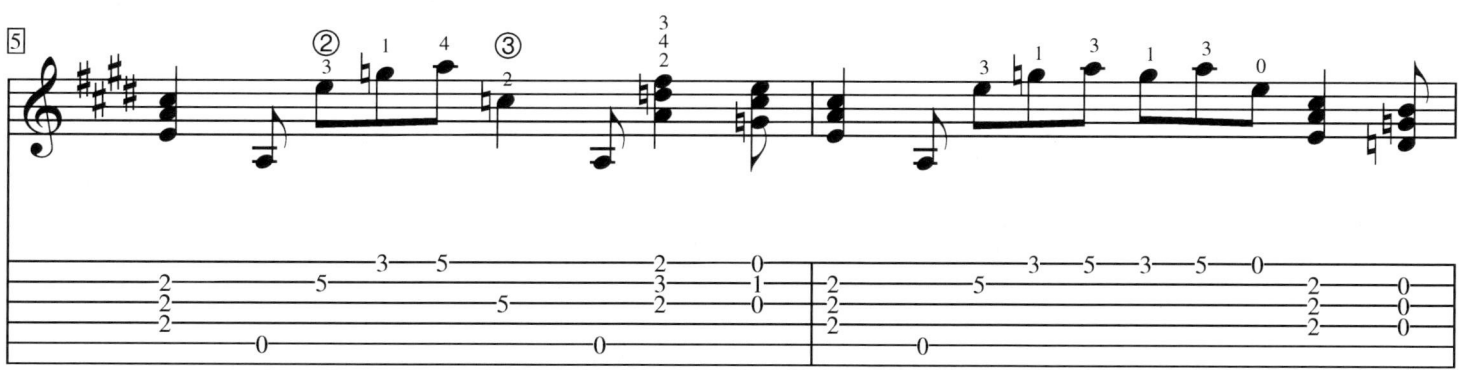

© 2004 by Mel Bay Publications, Inc. All Rights Reserved.

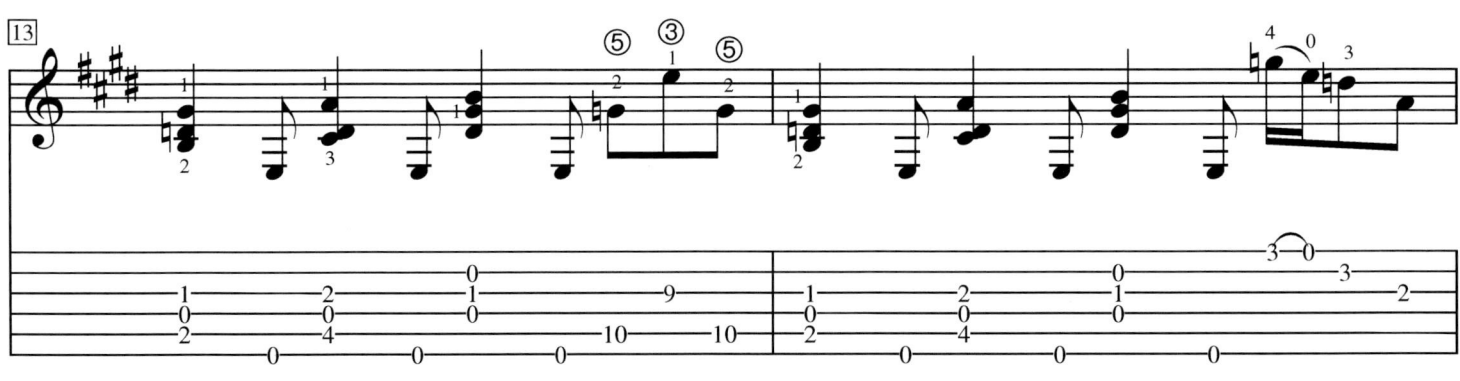

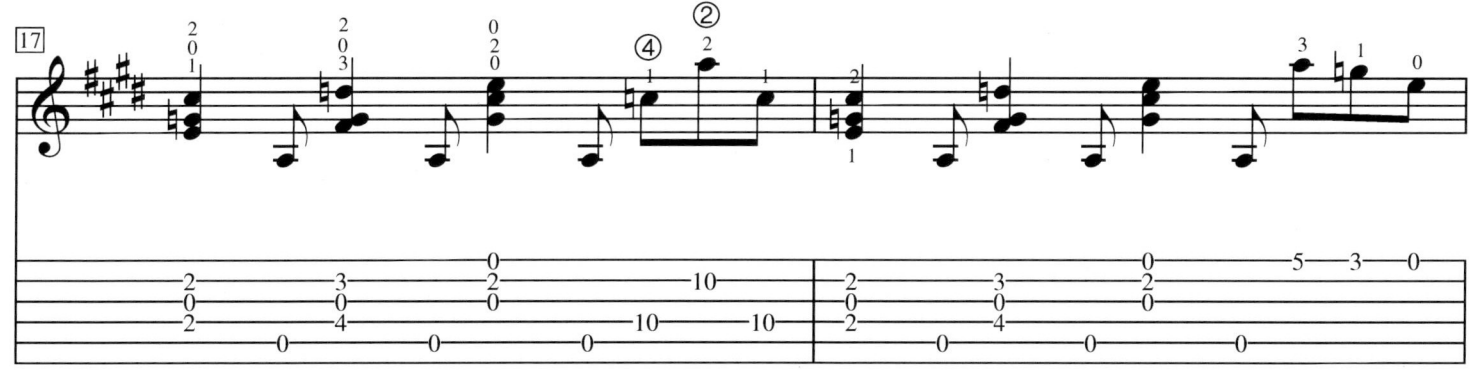
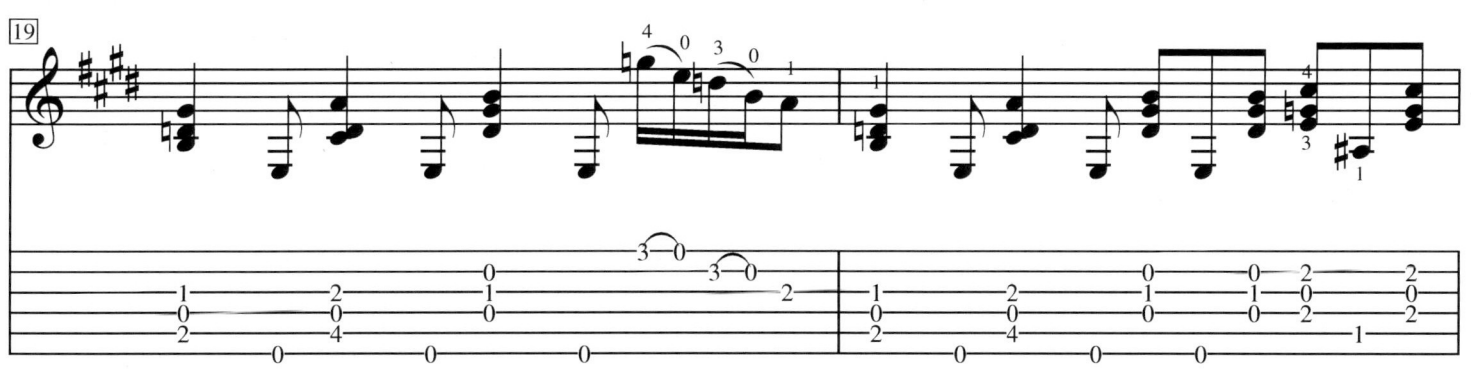
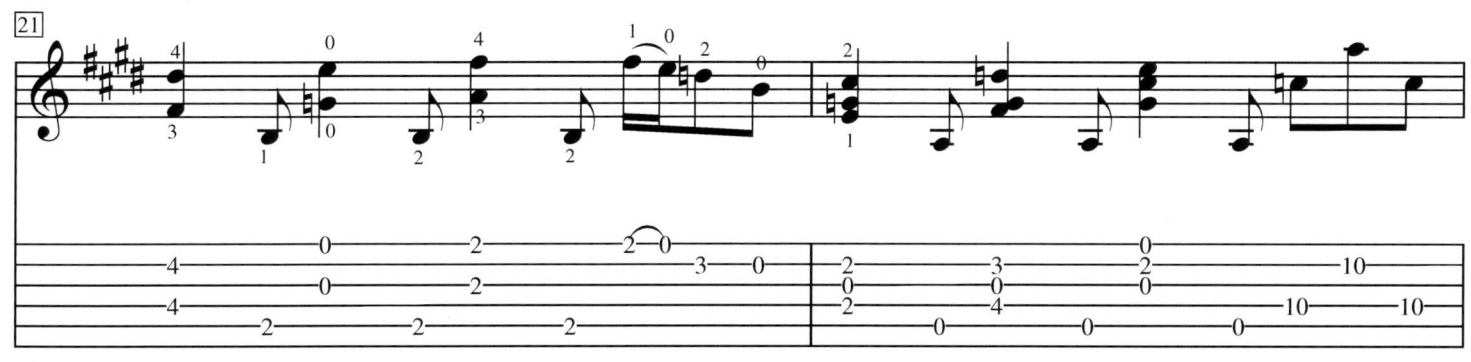

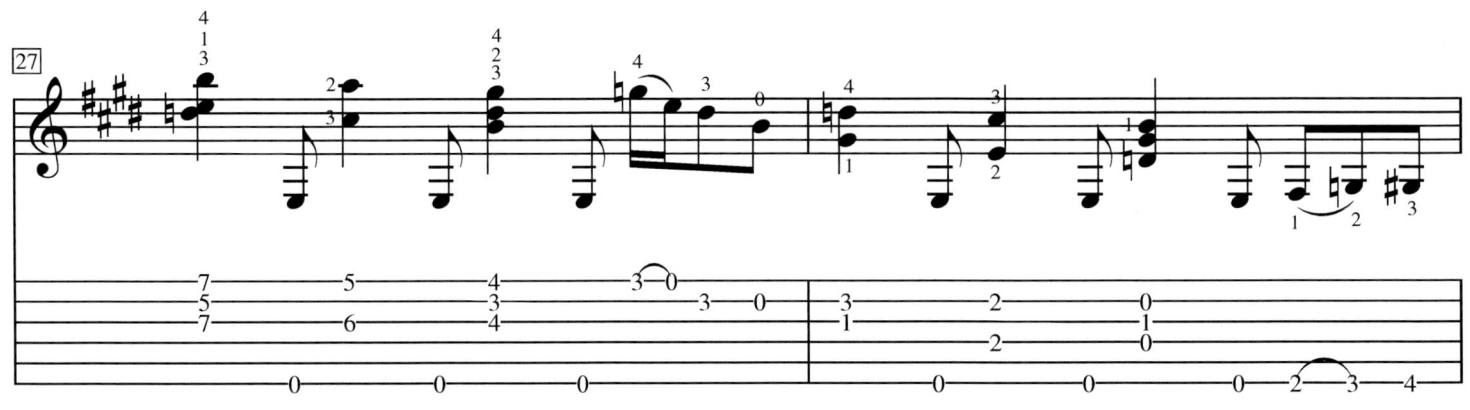
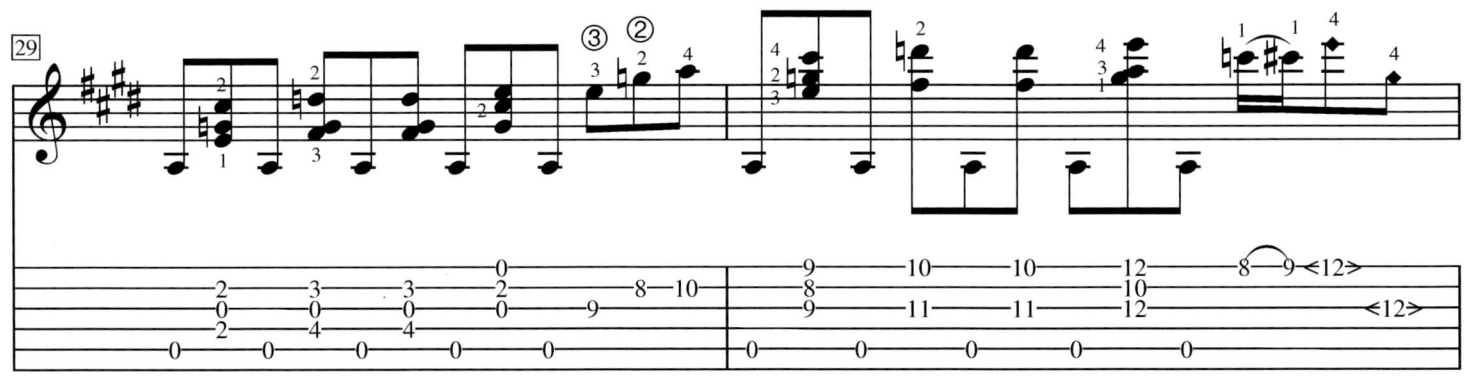

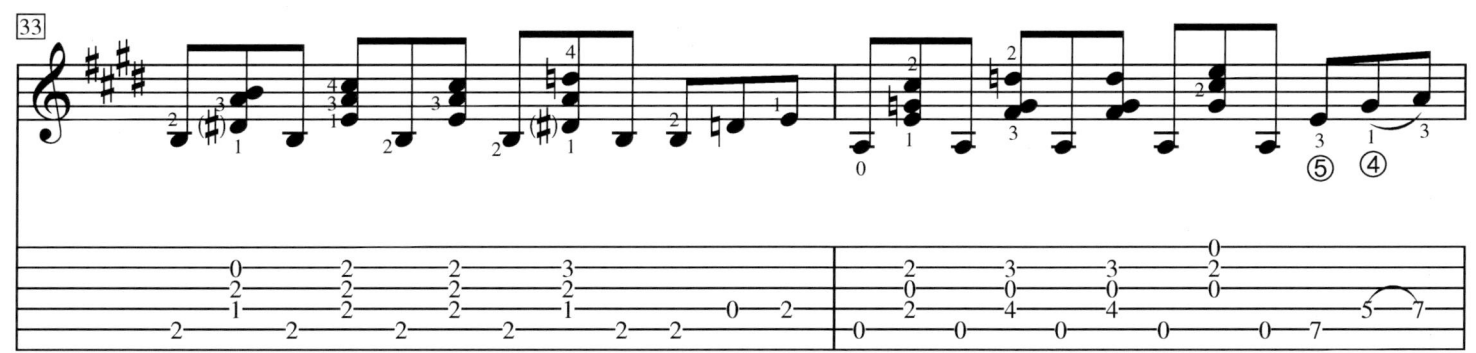
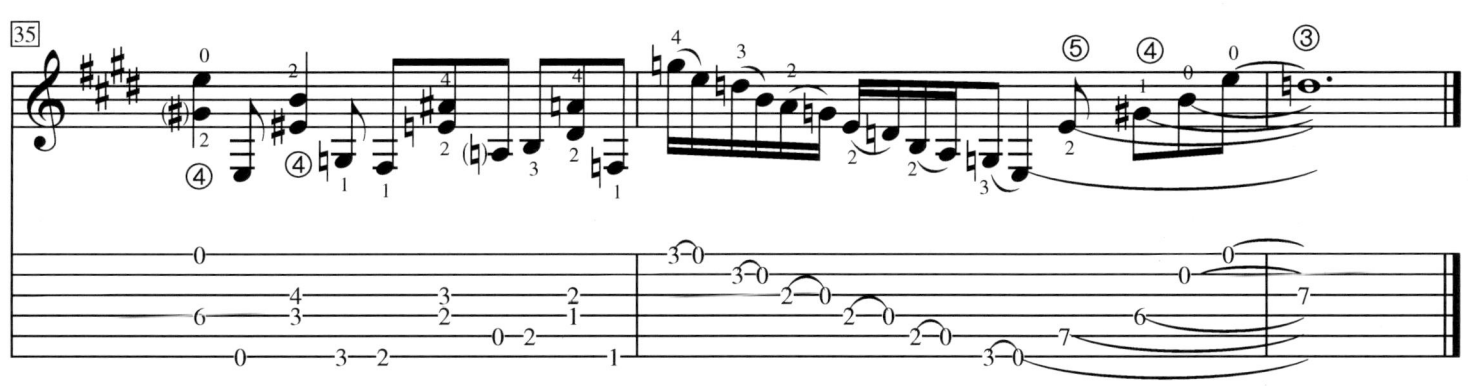

About the Author

William Beauvais has been commissioned to write for the Royal Conservatory Children's Choir, the Canadian Music Centre, Philip Candelaria, Jeffrey McFadden, the Evergreen Club, and the Echo Women's Choir. His music has been heard across Canada, the United States, Denmark, and most recently in Chile, Argentina and Uruguay. His guitar music is recorded on 2 compact discs: TRACES [1996] and bridges [1994]. An associate of the Canadian Music Centre and a member of the guitar faculty of The Royal Conservatory of Music, Beauvais is an accomplished classical guitarist. He won first prizes at the Canadian Music Competition, and at the Martinique world Centre for Guitar. He is presently developing curriculum for group based learning system at the Royal Conservatory in Toronto. His music is published by: Mel Bay, Frederick Harris, Editions d'Oz, and Tuscany Publications

WWW.MELBAY.COM